Helping
Kids
Through
Tough Times

Helping Kids Through Tough Times

Doris Sanford

Illustrated by Graci Evans

STANDARD
PUBLISHING
Cincinnati, Ohio

Edited by Henrietta Gambill
Illustrated by Graci Evans
Book Design by Bob Korth

Library of Congress Cataloging-in-Publication Data

Sanford, Doris
    Helping kids through tough times/by Doris Sanford; illustrated by Graci Evans
        p.   cm.
    ISBN 0-7847-0393-0
    1. Christian education of children. 2. Church work with children. 3. Children—Religious life. 4. Children—Conduct of life.
    I. Title.
    BV1475.2.S26   1995   95-8639
    259'.22—dc20   CIP

The Standard Publishing Company, Cincinnati, Ohio
A division of Standex International Corporation
© 1995 by Doris Sanford
All rights reserved
Printed in the United States of America
02 01 00 99 98 97 96 95   5 4 3 2 1

This book is dedicated with respect and gratitude to Tim Sanford.

SUBJECTS

Abortion

Adoption

AIDS

Alcoholic Parent

Alzheimer's

Attention Deficit Hyperactivity
    Disorder

Chronically Ill Child

Chronically Ill Parent

Critically Ill Parent

Cults

Death

Depressed Adult

Divorce

Drug Abuse

Eating Disorders

Emotional Abuse

Euthanasia

Failure

Fear

Foster Care

Gangs

Homosexual

Hospitalized Child

Latchkey Child

Loneliness

Mentally Ill Adult

Mental Retardation

Money

Moving

Murder

Natural Disasters

New Age

Occult

Overweight

Parental Fighting

Pet Death

Physical Disability

Poverty

Prejudice

Self-esteem, Low

Seriously Ill Child

Sexual Abuse, Boy

Sexual Abuse, Girl

Sexual Abuse, Protection
        Against

Single Parent

Stepparent

Suicide

Unemployment

Unwed Pregnancy

Violence on TV

The child who wants to understand

ABORTION

Understanding the Child

Children are exposed to controversial information about abortion through the media, seeing people picketing at abortion clinics, discussions at school, and perhaps through hearing conversations at home about abortion.

Young children are frightened by graphic descriptions of how abortions take place, but they do need to understand that a planned abortion is choosing to end the life of an unborn baby.

Children trust adults to provide for them and protect them, and it is scary when they understand that some adults choose to cause an unborn baby to die.

Adults must make it clear to children that it is wrong to kill abortion doctors because they kill babies when performing abortions.

Children should be informed about the efforts by their parents to combat abortion, such as letters to legislators or newspapers, prayer, and the support of pro-life movements. It is too simple to leave children believing that women who have abortions are unfeeling about their babies. Although women who have abortions usually feel some relief when the abortion is over, most will also feel sad, and many women will have painful feelings for many years after the abortion.

It is important to tell children that abortion is not against the law but that some laws need to be changed.

Since one of the ways that pro-abortion advocates support their position is denying the person-hood of the unborn baby, it helps for children to hear about the developing fetus through pregnancy, for example, when the heart is beating, when the baby has fingernails, etc.

What YOU Can Do to Help the Child

1. Children need to be told why the parents object to abortion and to hear Scripture verses that support this belief.
2. Children need to balance respect, kindness, and love for those who support abortion, and at the same time stand up for what they believe is right.
3. Children need to know that all people are loved by God, including people who do abortions, and women who have them.
4. Children can be included in supporting pro-life ministries by accompanying parents in taking baby supplies to unwed mothers who choose to keep their babies.
5. It is helpful to remind children that people who support abortions and people who oppose them are all sinners who need God's forgiveness.
6. Specific questions about how abortions are done can be answered with the briefest accurate answer possible. Let children decide if they want more information but don't impose it.
7. It is helpful for parents to tell children how happy they felt when they were pregnant with them and to describe the first kicks, growing tummy, etc.
8. Adults should ask children what they know about abortion before giving them information.
9. Children can be told the alternatives available to a pregnant woman who is unable or unwilling to parent a baby, i.e. adoption, and parenting classes to learn skills.

Conversation Starters

"If you heard about someone considering an abortion, you might suggest they talk to someone at a pro-life organization first. Would you know how to find one?"

"Why do you think some women choose to have an abortion?"

"Do you think a woman should have the right to choose to have an abortion? Why or why not?"

"What would Jesus do about abortion?"

"Why do you think abortion is wrong?"

"What have you heard about abortion?"

"Some people who support the right to abortion believe that the unborn baby doesn't feel any pain. That's not true. When babies are born at the same age that abortions are allowed, they respond to pain. Would you like some help in writing a report for school on why we believe abortion is wrong?"

Pointing the Child to God
Children need to know that God knew their name before they were born and had a plan for their life.

WHY IS ABORTION WRONG?

Why Is This So Hard?

Just because something is legal in our country, it doesn't make it right. The way we know if something is right or not is what God says about it. God says that He forms a baby in its mother's uterus before it is born. God even knows the baby's name before the baby is born!

Many people have very strong feelings about abortion. People who believe that abortion is right are called pro-choice, and people who believe that abortion is wrong are called pro-life.

There is no difference in a baby one day before it is born and one day after it is born. Killing an unborn baby is murder.

How Do Other Kids Feel?

Most kids feel angry and confused about why some grown-ups believe abortion is a woman's choice. Kids know that abortion is about the baby, not the mother, and nobody asked the baby if it wanted to be aborted. Most kids think that abortion is murder. It is hard for kids to understand that some laws are wrong because they can usually trust laws to protect them, but the abortion law allows babies to die. It is hard for kids to understand that even when someone is doing something wrong, such as people who support abortion, that Christians must not be rude or unkind.

This is how I feel

_____

_____

_____

_____

I Can Help Myself

1. I can pray for women who are considering having abortions and for the doctors and nurses who do abortions.
2. I can thank God that my parents gave me the gift of life.
3. I can ask my parents how to express my beliefs without showing bad manners.
4. I can tell my friends what I believe about abortion and why I believe it.
5. I can march in pro-life parades with my parents.

I Can Make Good Choices

1. I can write a letter to the political leaders of my country and tell them how I feel about abortion.
2. I can read the Bible verses that tell how God feels about unborn babies, including how God felt about me before I was born.
3. I can ask my parents the questions I have about abortion.
4. I can look up the names of adoption agencies in the phone book and remember there are lots of parents who would like to adopt a newborn baby.
5. I can ask my parents to show me the pro-life office nearest our home.

I Can Trust God To Be There For Me

Bible Verse: "Before I formed you in the womb I knew you, before you were born I set you apart" (Jeremiah 1:5).

Prayer: Dear God, thank you that you love us from the minute we are conceived. Please help us stop abortions in the world. Amen.

The **ADOPTED** child

Understanding the Child

The concerns of adopted children vary depending on the child's age at the time of adoption, the personality of the particular child, the amount of open discussion about the circumstances of the adoption, whether or not there was a strong bond to the biological parents prior to the adoption, whether the child experienced other emotional trauma prior to the adoption, and a multitude of other factors. No two children will respond in exactly the same way, even if they are siblings with similar life experiences. And, even if adoptive parents do everything right, most adopted children will need to address the fact of their adoption and make peace with it.

The questions and concerns adopted children face are often linked to the child's developmental stage. The preschool child may be trying to understand that she grew in another mommy's tummy. The school-age child may be curious about characteristics of the biological parent (rich or talented?). And the adolescent may wonder why the biological parent relinquished them for adoption, and whether the parent misses them.

It is not uncommon for children to develop fantasies about their biological parents in order to fill in the missing pieces of unknown information.

In addition to common questions, some of the stress adopted children face is caused by overhearing insensitive remarks of curious adults, i.e.

"Couldn't you have children of your own?"
"He doesn't look like your other kids."
"Why didn't his parents keep him?"

All of these remarks reinforce the core issue of adoption, which is, that no matter how loved the adopted child is, sooner or later he needs to accept the fact that to be adopted, he must first have been released by hisbiological parents.

What YOU Can Do to Help the Adopted Child

1. Children need to hear about the adoption from their parents. Most authorities believe that the word "adoption" should be used casually and with smiles from the time the child enters the home. To delay telling the child until he can really understand, is to risk breaking trust with the child, i.e. if my parents didn't tell me about this, are they withholding other information?
2. Don't expect the older adopted child to bond instantly even if they have been removed from an abusive biological home. Trust must be earned slowly.
3. It takes time for older adopted children to feel that they belong in the family as much as the biological children, and to build genuine sibling relationships with the other children.
4. Expect to talk about the adoption at each developmental stage in the child's life from preschool to adulthood.
5. The way a parent talks about the adoption is as important as the content of what is said. Animated excitement or tears of joy will communicate pleasure in ways that words cannot.
6. Don't tell the child he was given away.
7. Don't make negative statements about the birth parents. The child's identity will always be attached to the birth parents, no matter how difficult that relationship might have been or how wonderful the adoptive parents are.
8. Don't tell adopted children they are special because they were adopted, since birth children will wonder if they are less special.

Conversation Starters

"Whenever you want to hear about how you came into our family, please ask. We will tell you as often as you want to hear it."

"I bet that one of your birth parents had musical talent because you are so gifted."

"We know that you love your birth parents. You don't have to be uncomfortable talking about it because we also know that you love us."

"Your dad and I don't talk about your adoption to the children in our new neighborhood because we want you to decide who and when kids should be told."

"Do you think about your birth family?"

Pointing the Child to God

Children need to know that everyone who accepts Jesus is adopted by Him.

AM I ADOPTED?

Why Is It So Hard?

Nothing about you caused your birth parents to be unable to take care of you. You were a sweet, wonderful child, and your adoptive parents feel very happy to have you for their child! Your birth parents wanted the best for you.

When you were adopted, your adoptive parents made a promise to take care of you until you are grown up. They signed a legal paper which stated that you are permanently a part of the family.

Most kids have questions about their adoption. It's okay to ask any question about adoption. Your adoptive parents may not know all of the answers about your birth family, but they will understand your need to ask.

How Do Other Adopted Kids Feel?

When kids are little, it may be hard for them to understand that they have two sets of parents. Kids are curious about their birth parents and like to have their questions answered. Asking questions about their biological parents doesn't mean that they are not happy in their adoptive home. Kids who are adopted by parents of another race are usually glad when they can spend time with people of their own race and learn about their heritage. Some kids worry that their adoptive parents might be mad at their biological parents. Some kids have "open adoptions" which means that their birth parents and adoptive parents meet and talk about the adoption. Sometimes kids continue to see their birth parents after they are adopted.

This is how I feel

_____

_____

_____

_____

I Can Help Myself

1. I can read books from the library about adopted children so I will understand how other kids think and feel.
2. I can remember that being loved by my family doesn't depend on how I entered it.
3. I can forgive my birth parents for not being able to take care of me and be thankful that they allowed me to be adopted.
4. I can show respect for my adoptive parents and acknowledge that they have the responsibility to discipline me.

I Can Make Good Choices

1. I can learn how to respond when others ask personal questions about the adoption.
2. I can love both my birth parents for giving me life and my adoptive parents for giving me a family.
3. If I am worried about hurting my adoptive parents' feelings when I talk about my birth family, I can ask them how they feel and tell them how much I love them.
4. I choose to believe that I am loved and lovable.

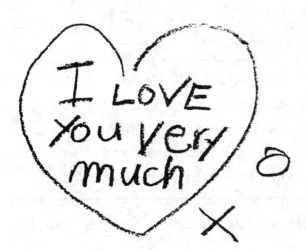

I Can Trust God to Be There for Me

Bible Verse: "In love he predestined us to be adopted as his sons through Jesus Christ" (Ephesians 1:5).

Prayer: Dear God, thank you for adopting me into your family, and thank you that my parents adopted me into our family. Amen.

The child who knows someone with

AIDS

Understanding the Child

No amount of accurate factual information about
AIDS will completely protect the child from the
stigma that is attached to this disease. Some of
the hurt that the child will experience will be the
result of the judgment and lack of acceptance by
others, not the direct impact of the disease itself.
Children are sometimes told not to tell anyone
about the diagnosis of AIDS. This shame and
secrecy will reinforce the unacceptable nature of
the illness.

Children who live in a family with someone with
AIDS, have likely observed years of gradually
increasing physical illnesses in the person with
AIDS. The child may not have known that these
diseases were caused by the AIDS virus, however.
Children are often shocked and uncomfortable
when they are told.

Children are given information about HIV disease in public school, including safe-
guards that protect children from acquiring the virus. Very young children can
learn to practice universal precautions. Children may wonder why an adult would
participate in a high-risk activity that could result in acquiring the AIDS virus.

The average life expectancy following the diagnosis of AIDS is ten or more years.
Chronic grief, worry, sadness accompany the roller-coaster of wellness alternating
with the crisis of a new infection. Children live with fear and tension.

Persons with AIDS often have multiple caregivers, such as hospice workers, non
family caregivers, representatives from community AIDS organizations, visiting
friends, etc. All of these people add to the confusion of living in a family with
someone with AIDS.

What YOU Can Do to Help the Child

1. Establish a consistent routine for the child to minimize the disruption of the crises and plateaus of the illness.

2. Answer questions honestly about how the disease was acquired in the simplest way possible. Explain homosexuality by saying, "He got it from another person with the AIDS virus." Children do not need personal information about sexual practices about homosexuals anymore than they do about heterosexuals.

3. Model loving, accepting attitudes toward the person with AIDS. It will be more important than anything that is said.

4. Include children in assisting in the care of persons with AIDS so they do not feel helpless. Children can help decorate rooms, color pictures, or make cookies for the person with AIDS.

5. In explaining why the person participated in an activity that could give them the HIV virus, say that they may not have known it was an unsafe activity or they may have thought that they wouldn't get it, even if they were doing something unsafe.

6. Talk to children about God's acceptance of all of us and that we are all sinners in need of God's mercy.

7. Be clear about how the virus is spread and what is safe and unsafe for the child to do. Tell children that they can't tell by looking at someone whether they have the virus.

8. Let children decide how much time they want to spend with the person with AIDS. Allow they to visit or not visit the person.

9. Prepare children for the stigma attached to a diagnosis of AIDS, and define the correct Christian response, for example, say that loving and helping a person with AIDS does not mean we support using IV drugs.

Conversation Starters

> "Yes, your daddy and I are divorced, but that doesn't mean you can't tell me how badly you feel about his HIV disease. I know that you love him."

> "Let's practice some ways you could respond if someone asks you how Uncle Derek got AIDS."

> "If someone asks you to do something that you know would not make God happy, what would you say?"

> "What have you learned about AIDS?"

> "I am feeling very sad right now. How do you feel?"

Pointing the Child to God

Children need to know that there will be many people in heaven who died from AIDS. God loves and forgives anyone who is sorry for their sins and asks for forgiveness, and many people were infected when they have done nothing wrong to acquire the virus.

THE SCARIEST DISEASE IN THE WORLD

Why Does This Hurt So Much?

If you know someone with AIDS, you have probably felt the worry and fear that people in your family are feeling. Maybe you have been to the hospital at times to visit this person when they have had a new illness, and that was scary, too. It is okay to be worried when you don't know what will happen next.

Another reason that this is hard is that grandparents may be especially upset and unable to help you like they used to do.

How Do Other Kids Feel?

Most kids are not sure who they can talk to about what is happening in their family. They don't tell their friends because they are afraid friends will think they can catch AIDS just by coming over to play.

Kids might wonder if the person with AIDS is being punished by God. The answer is no. AIDS is a disease that people get by doing something that gives them the virus.

Usually kids who know someone with AIDS understand a lot more about the disease than kids who have never known anyone with the disease. Sometimes it feels good to give others information about AIDS so they know the truth.

This is how I feel

_____

_____

_____

_____

I Can Make Good Choices

1. I can offer to help the person with AIDS by reading to him, telling him good jokes, bringing him a cold drink, playing games, and by saying, "I love you."
2. I will never touch the blood of another person or any body fluids without wearing gloves. If someone is hurt, I will ask an adult to help him. I won't pick up a dirty syringe.
3. I can role play ways to say "no" to a person who asks me to do something that I know is not safe.
4. I will remember that how a person got the disease has nothing to do with the way I am to treat them.

I Can Help Myself

1. I can read one of the pamphlets, written for children, with AIDS information so I can get my questions answered.
2. It's okay to play and have fun and go to my friends' houses. I don't have to think about AIDS all of the time.
3. I can decide who I want to tell that there is a person with AIDS in my family. I don't have to tell everybody.
4. If people ask me questions that are private, I can say "That is something just for my family to know."

I Can Trust God to Be There for Me

Bible Verse: "We all, like sheep, have gone astray, each of us has turned to his own way; and the Lord has laid on him the iniquity of us all" (Isaiah 53:6).

Prayer: Dear God, I know that you love people with AIDS as much as you love me. Help me to love the people who judge and condemn people with AIDS, too. Amen.

The child living with an
ALCOHOLIC

Understanding the Child

Many children live with an alcoholic. It is estimated
that approximately one in five children live in a home
with someone who abuses alcohol. The needs of the
alcoholic are often more important than those of
anyone else in the family.

Children believe that whatever is happening in their
home is normal. They are usually loyal and protective
of the family and are not likely to talk about the family
problems. Denial is learned early.

Children adapt to their circumstances by assuming a
particular role in the family: sometimes "parenting"
the adults, sometimes defusing tension by acting like
a clown, or at times by being rebellious.

Children don't know that the nonalcoholic parent
may be preoccupied with the alcoholic parent's
behavior. The non drinking parent may be as sick as
the alcoholic.

Children grow up believing that it is unacceptable
to talk about feelings or even to feel their hurt and
loneliness. Children are praised for their adult-like
behavior and for denying that life is difficult for them.

Home may be filled with chaos, disorganization, and
unpredictable punishment. Children are scolded for
behavior that is ignored the next week.

Children frequently do not understand that alcoholism is a disease, and that their alcoholic parent
cannot stop drinking without treatment.

What **YOU** Can Do to Help the Child

1. Spend time playing with the child. Don't praise adult-like behavior.
2. Offer your emotional warmth, nurture, and comfort. Provide parenting by guidance, direction, and encouragement.
3. Give children factual information about alcoholism. If you don't have the facts, get printed material from Alcoholics Anonymous.
4. Teach children how to express feelings. Use "feeling" words in your conversation. Tell children how other children feel.
5. Do not criticize the alcohol abusing parent. If you are angry or disgusted, you will be rejected by the child.
6. Children need permission to be happy even if their parent does not stop drinking. Tell children that they cannot make their parent stop drinking, and they are not responsible for the problems in their home.
7. Tell children that even if the alcoholic parent goes to Alcoholics Anonymous for help, they may initially be gone to AA meetings as much as when they were gone to bars.
8. Teach children appropriate social skills and behavior. Many children of alcoholics do not know how to behave in public, how to make friends, etc.
9. Children need to know what to do to protect themselves in emergencies. What to do if the alcoholic parent passes out and is bleeding, or if the house is locked when they come home, or if they are left stranded without a ride home after a school event.

Conversation Starters

"When you feel worried or afraid, you can tell me and I will help you. Here is twenty-five cents. Call me from a pay phone if you need help with a problem."

"Our family is going to the beach for the weekend. Would you like to go with us?"

"Would you like to come over to my house and do some jobs to earn your own spending money?"

"Do you know any other kids who live with an alcoholic parent?"

"I know that your dad is an alcoholic. So was my dad when I was little. Can I tell you what it was like for me to live with my alcoholic parent?"

Pointing the Child to God

Children need to know that God can help people who want to stop abusing alcohol. And, that children of alcoholics deserve help because they are precious to God.

"What do you think is the hardest thing for kids who live with an alcoholic?"

LIVING WITH AN ALCOHOLIC IS AWFUL!

Why Does This Hurt So Much?

If you are living with an alcoholic, you might feel angry, confused, sad, and frightened. Most children of alcoholics don't feel very good about themselves and think that they have caused their parent to abuse alcohol. Of course that isn't true. Maybe there have been times when you did not get the clothes or supplies you needed because the money had been spent on alcohol. Or, perhaps you had to ride in a car with a drunk parent and you felt very scared. One of the hardest experiences for children who live with an alcoholic parent is their parents loud fighting. Maybe you have been embarrassed by your alcoholic parent's behavior in front of your friends. These experiences also happen for many other children too. No wonder living with an alcoholic hurts so much!

How Do Other Kids Feel?

Living with an alcoholic is a big problem for kids, but sometimes kids have a hard time talking about it because they feel ashamed. Of course it is never the child's fault if a parent abuses alcohol, but most kids don't know that at first.

Kids feel frustrated when they are accused by an alcoholic parent of doing something they didn't do, or when they are punished for doing something they were told to do. Alcoholic parents have very poor memories caused by black outs.

It is hard to listen to a nonalcoholic parent lie to protect the alcoholic parent. Telling the boss that daddy has the flu, instead of a hangover, for example.

This is how I feel _____

_____

_____

_____

I Can Make Good Choices

1. I can choose to be happy even if my parent doesn't stop drinking.
2. I can choose not to abuse alcohol when I am an adult because I know I might have been born with the potential to be an alcoholic, too.
3. I can choose to talk about my family problems. If there is a support group at school, I can join it.
4. I can learn to ride the bus in case I need transportation.

I Can Help Myself

1. I can talk to a kind, understanding adult and tell the truth about what is happening in my home.
2. I can write down the rules in case my alcoholic parent denies what was said.
3. I can spend time playing with friends who like me.
4. I can quit trying to fix my alcoholic parent, stop counting drinks, hiding bottles, making excuses, or pretending alcohol is not a problem.
5. I can plan what to do if I feel unsafe at home, such as go to a neighbor's house and ask for help.

I Can Trust God to Be There for Me

Bible Verse: "Cast all your anxiety on him because he cares for you" (1 Peter 5:7).

Prayer: Dear God, sometimes I feel scared. I know that you know everything that is happening in my family. Please help me and help my parents turn to you. Amen.

Understanding the Child

The impact on the child of knowing and loving a grandparent with Alzheimer's will vary depending on the unique relationship of the child to the grandparent, how much time the child has spent with her, and how old the child is at the time symptoms begin.

Even when children are not emotionally close to the grandparent, they will sense the increasing stress that the illness creates for adults in the family.

Children have difficulty understanding chronic illness and tend to assume that's the way Grandpa acts, rather than that the behavior is a direct result of Alzheimer's. For that matter, symptoms are usually so slow in developing that adults may not understand the problem initially themselves.

There are several family crises common to Alzheimer's which have deep impact on children. The grandparent with Alzheimer's may need to leave his own home and move in with the child's family, and since this disease is progressive, the grandparent will eventually die.

Parents of the child may initially deny that there is a medical problem out of fear that the disease is hereditary, and because the disease is so overwhelming.

Children who have had a close relationship with the grandparent will experience increasing loss and grief, as the grandparent withdraws more and more due to the illness. Since dementia often causes outbursts of anger, children may be the recipients of undeserved attacks of hostility.

What YOU Can Do to Help the Child

1. Don't protect children from the truth when the cause of the behavior is known. "Grandma will probably die from Alzheimer's, but it may be a long time from now."
2. Encourage children to express their sadness as they mourn the loss of a special relationship to the grandparent.
3. Tell the child what to do when she receives angry verbal outbursts from the grandparent, i.e. she should tell you and you will comfort her.
4. Protect children from the embarrassment of the grandparent undressing in front of the child's friends. Closely supervise the grandparent when friends visit.
5. Explain developing symptoms as they occur; tell the child the name of the illness; explain what the family will do to help the person with Alzheimer's.
6. Clearly define what the child is and is not responsible to do in providing care for the grandparent. Children need permission to play without feeling guilty.
7. Do not tolerate behaviors that make fun of the symptoms of the sick person, but do encourage a good sense of humor about problems. Laugh with and not at the sick person.
8. Parents who take care of a grandparent will be less and less available to focus on the child. Other adults can spend time playing with the child.
9. Prepare children for alterations in scheduled events. The parent may not be able to take the child to a play if the grandparent experiences an abrupt change in behavior.
   If family meal times are spoiled by the behavior of the grandparent, the grandparent may need to be fed at a different time than the rest of the family.

Conversation Starters

"Tonight we will have a family meeting and talk about what we can do to help Grandma. Do you have some ideas you want to share?"

"When Grandpa gets up at night and wanders around the house, your dad or I will get up to help him. That's not your job. Is there anything else you are worried about?"

"I noticed that Grandma yelled at you. It must have hurt your feelings. Would you like to talk about it?"

"We really appreciate your help, but now it is time for you to go play and have fun. Would you like to invite someone over?

Pointing the Child to God

Children need to know that God asks us to be kind even when the other person is not kind to us, and that He will help us obey Him.

WHO CAN I TELL ABOUT ALZHEIMER'S?

Why Is This So Hard?

Maybe you are feeling really confused and worried about what is happening to someone that you love. Usually older people don't get brain diseases, so you may not have expected this to happen in your family. Maybe you don't know if it is okay to tell your friends about the problem. Usually it helps to tell others that the behavior is caused by a disease called Alzheimer's. That way, they will understand.

Maybe you feel mad because your grand-parent accused you of taking money from him, and you know you didn't. That is one of the symptoms of Alzheimer's. Just explain that it didn't really happen.

How Do Other Kids Feel?

Kids have a hard time understanding why a grown-up does a dangerous activity like wandering into the street. Kids who live with someone with Alzheimer's usually have to help protect the grown-up.

Kids feel sad because their parents may be so busy taking care of the person with Alzheimer's that they don't have as much time for them.

Kids wonder if they will get Alzheimer's when they get old. The answer is, probably they won't.

This is how I feel

_____

_____

_____

_____

I Can Help Myself

1. I will remember that my grandparent helped me when I was a baby and now it is my turn to help her.
2. I can show love and kindness. It will help my grandparent, and it will make me feel good, too.
3. When my grandparent doesn't remember my name anymore, I will know that it's the disease that made him forget.
4. I can ask questions about dementia. The more I know the easier it will be for me.
5. I can tell my friends that my grandparent has a brain disease, and tell them what he was like before he got sick.

I Can Make Good Choices

1. I can remember that I am an important helper. I can pick flowers, sing a song, or change the calendar every day so my grandparent knows what day it is.
2. I can be patient. I know my grandparent can't remember what I have said.
3. If anyone makes fun of my grandparent, I will tell them about Alzheimer's. I could give a report about it at school.
4. If my grandparent follows me around I can go outside and play, or talk to my parents and ask for their help.
5. I will watch my grandparent in the kitchen so he doesn't eat something harmful or hurt himself.

I Can Trust God to Be There for Me

Bible Verse: "He who is kind to the poor lends to the Lord, and he will reward him for what he has done" (Proverbs 19:17).

Prayer: Dear God, thank you for being kind to me and sending Jesus to be my Savior. I want to show kindness to others, especially my grandparent. Amen.

The **ATTENTION DEFICIT HYPERACTIVE** Child

Understanding the Child

The behaviors associated with ADHD may be present in a child as young as four years, although most children are not diagnosed with this disorder until they attend school where a teacher observes that the child can't seem to finish things he starts, is easily distracted, has a tendency to leap before he looks, talks out of turn, calls out answers in class at inappropriate times, does messy work, interrupts others, loses his belongings, fails to follow game rules, has difficulty getting along with other children, and feels badly about himself.

Children with ADHD receive poor grades in school, but they are not stupid. Many children with ADHD are exceptionally bright. They talk constantly. They can't sit through a meal. They are children who are in constant undirected motion: walking, climbing, running, fidgeting, and squirming.

Sitting quietly for these children is cruel (but not unusual) punishment. ADHD is suspected of being an inherited medical disorder, not a psychological one. Children may have attention deficit without being hyperactive. These children are not deliberate trouble makers, and they cannot change their behavior simply by trying harder.

Boys are five times more likely to have ADHD than girls. Girls with the problem are more inclined to daydream and have attention deficit without hyperactivity.

Parents of children with Attention Deficit Hyperactivity Disorder are criticized for being lazy, not making the child mind and being bad parents. Both children and their parents need acceptance, support, and information.

What **YOU** Can Do to Help the Child With ADHD

1. Respect, value, honor the child. Recognize that the disability makes life difficult for the child.
2. Use as many simple visual aids as possible. Don't just tell the child, show him. State directions as clearly as possible, and give only one direction at a time.
3. It is not helpful to punish children with ADHD by spanking them. They respond better to being deprived of privileges for a short duration.
4. When children are in groups, place the child close to the adult and away from distractions. This will allow access for extra help as needed.
5. Encourage and compliment children at every opportunity.
6. Trust and value parent's advice regarding how to help the child away from home.
7. Have fun with the ADHD child.
8. Maintain a predictable routine schedule at home. Post the times of day for events. Have a set time to do homework, chores, go to bed, etc.
9. Require respect from peers. Explain the disorder to friends with the child's permission.
10. Give the child opportunities for success, not failure. Don't expect behavior that is unreasonable.
11. Seek skilled medical advice from practitioners who work frequently with ADHD. Join an ADHD parent support group.
12. Don't pressure a child to make decisions. Narrow them down to one or two choices and then let him decide.
13. Children with ADHD forget easily. Remind them in non demeaning ways.

Conversation Starters

"You are very smart. Your learning disability makes it hard for you to learn. May I show you one thing that I think will help you?"

"What kind of art projects do you especially enjoy?"

"Tell me what you know about ADHD? About your medication?"

"He said that you are not paying attention. In fact you are paying too much attention to too many things. May I teach him about ADHD?"

"I noticed that you didn't interrupt while she was talking."

"I like the way you are learning to control your behavior."

Pointing the Child to God

Children need to know that God wants them to use their lives to do good, whether they have a learning disability or not.

I WISH I COULD PAY ATTENTION!

Why Is This So Hard?

Maybe you have heard someone say that if you would just pay attention you would be just fine. But sometimes you can't pay attention because you have a learning disability, just like a kid who is blind and can't see. Learning disabilities are nobody's fault. Sometimes they are inherited. It never happens because someone is lazy or bad or undisciplined or mentally retarded or spoiled.

Kids with a learning disability often have a hard time at school, although they are just as smart or maybe even smarter than other kids. Attention Deficit Hyperactivity Disorder is not something you outgrow, but you can learn how to manage it better so that life is easier for you.

How Do Other Kids Feel?

Most kids with Attention Deficit Hyperactivity Disorder have a hard time feeling good about themselves because they are frequently in trouble at school, at home, or with their friends. Lots of kids don't know what is expected of them or how they are supposed to act. Kids with ADHD forget what they have been told and need to learn ways to remember the rules. Sometimes kids with ADHD sleep less than other kids, so if everybody in your family needs more sleep than you do, that could be a problem.

Kids with ADHD want a chance to succeed, not fail. They want encouragement to do the best they can, and they want to be loved and accepted like everybody else.

This is how I feel

_____

_____

_____

_____

I Can Help Myself

1. I can ask my parents if I can have a sticker chart for all of the things I do right.
2. I can ask a friend to work with me on projects for school, while I practice being patient and working cooperatively.
3. When someone is talking to me, I can learn to look at her in the eye. If I don't understand what she said, I can ask her to repeat it.
4. I can learn about Attention Deficit Hyperactivity Disorder and about my medication.

I Can Make Good Choices

1. I can volunteer to do things that I do well at school, such as make classroom displays, bulletin boards, or act in performances.
2. I can ask that family rules be posted at home so I can read them when I forget.
3. I can make lists of things I need to do and carry the list in my pocket. I will cross off things as I do them.
4. I can remember to take my turn when I am playing games with my friends. When I forget to do this, I can apologize.
5. I can read stories about all of the famous people in history who had Learning Disabilities, such as Albert Einstein and Thomas Edison.

I Can Trust God to Be There for Me

Bible Verse: " The fear of the Lord is the beginning of knowledge, but fools despise wisdom and discipline" (Proverbs 1:7).

Prayer: Dear God, I want to learn more about you, and to obey you. I forget easily. Please help me. Amen.

The **CHRONICALLY ILL** child

Understanding the Child

Children experience a variety of disorders that require lifetime medical intervention. Some are life threatening and others are not. Chronic illnesses in children include epilepsy, leukemia, asthma, diabetes and many others. Whatever the problem, children will need to make adjustments to the limitations imposed on them by their illness including doctor's visits, emergency hospitalizations during a crisis, regular medications (including injections and IV's).

Children with serious illness may be overly protected by their parents both with restrictions in their play (to prevent exposure to germs from other children), or by indulging the child in an effort to compensate for the discomfort and difficulty of the illness. Chronically ill children need the freedom to enjoy their childhood and to be held accountable for their behavior, just as any other child.

Parents may attempt to minimize the seriousness of the illness to the child. Denial seldom works, because children sense the fear of their parents whether or not it is acknowledged.

Very young children can learn to manage many of their home health needs and feel less dependent by doing so. They can give their own injections, stay within diet limits, use inhalers, test their blood sugar, etc. The more a child does for himself, the more he feels in control.

Children with chronic illness need to understand their illness and they need to know that there are many other children throughout the world who have the same problem.

Information may be obtained from the pediatrician or possibly through a national organization, such as the American Cancer Society that provides information and support for families.

What **YOU** Can Do to Help the Chronically Ill Child

1. Find creative ways to include children at school and church activities, provide non sweet treats for the diabetic child.

2. Learn the details of how to provide care for the child, so that parents can get away alone at times.

3. Communicate information to medical professionals that will assist them in being sensitive to the child, i.e. that he can hold still for the blood test if you let him tell you when he is ready.

4. Spend time with the other children in the family so they do not resent all of the adult attention the sick child receives.

5. With the permission of the parents gather pamphlets that provide information about the illness for families of the children the sick child plays with most.

6. Learn proper responses for common emergencies so that the parents feel safe allowing the child to be with you, i.e. what to do in an asthma attack, insulin reaction, or a seizure.

7. Don't give the child or his parents advice. Listen and help them sort through alternatives.

8. Provide consistent contact with the child. Many people are initially supportive but unavailable as the months and years pass.

9. Don't make the focus of your time with the child on the illness. Talk about ordinary things that interest the child, play and have fun.

Conversation Starters

"Please tell me if you need my help. Otherwise, I will assume that you are doing okay on your own."

"What do you wish other kids understood about Cystic Fibrosis?"

"Would you like to tell the teacher about your epilepsy or would you like me to do it?"

"If you could have one wish, what would it be?"

"What is the worst part about being sick?"

"Do other kids ever give you a bad time about being sick?"

Pointing the Child to God

Children need to know that God is close beside them when they are scared, and that He will never, ever leave them alone.

I WONDER IF I'LL EVER GET WELL

Why Does This Hurt So Much?

If you have a chronic illness, you are probably really tired of all of the ways that the illness affects your life. I bet you wish you didn't have to see the doctor so often or take treatments, or always have to remember to take your medicine. Who wouldn't be tired of all that!

Maybe you feel the worry of your parents and that makes you worried. Maybe you wonder what will happen next and that worries you, too. And, maybe you worry about having to go back into the hospital.

Some kids resent the restrictions that other kids don't have.

How Do Other Kids Feel?

Kids like to talk to other kids with the same illness. They don't feel so different when they talk to kids who have had many of the same experiences. They like to share funny stories about things that happened at the hospital, or tell about the trick they played on the doctor.

Kids also want to be accepted by other kids who are not sick. Kids know when they are more healthy than unhealthy, no matter how serious their medical problem is. They still want to hear good jokes, talk about sports and friends and homework, and what music they like best.

This is how I feel

_____

_____

_____

_____

I Can Help Myself

1. I can learn all I can about my illness, and I can ask the doctor any questions I have. I have a right to know.
2. I can decide which friends I want to tell about my illness. Not everyone needs to know about it.
3. I can ask the doctor or nurse to tell me if something is going to hurt. I don't like that kind of surprise!
4. I can learn to concentrate on something intently during a painful treatment or squeeze the hand of a grown-up.
5. I can express my feelings with clay or art.

I Can Make Good Choices

1. I can thank people who help me, and I can choose to be kind and polite to them even if they give me shots!
2. I can make a scrapbook of my hospital experiences with pictures of my doctors and nurses, autographs, menus, and the cards I received. I can write a journal of how I felt and what I thought during my stay at the hospital.
3. I can teach other kids at school about my illness by giving a report about it. If I tell them about it they won't be so afraid.
4. I can think happy thoughts and about becoming all that I can be.

I Can Trust God to Be There for Me

Bible Verse: "The Lord is my shepherd, I shall not be in want" (Psalm 23:1).

Prayer: Dear God, sometimes I get so tired of being sick. Thank you for loving me, helping me, cheering me on. Amen.

The child with a
CHRONICALLY ILL PARENT

Understanding the Child

The child who lives with a chronically parent will have a different childhood than the child who has healthy parents. Family life may revolve around the needs of the sick parent and children may be asked to adjust their needs again and again to accommodate to the more urgent needs of the ill parent.

Children may have less freedom to invite friends over to play at their home due to the additional noise and confusion that results. The time available for transporting the child to homes of other children or to church or school activity may be complicated by the necessity of the healthy parent to remain at home and provide care for the sick parent.

Children assume responsibility and therefore the guilt for problems that occur in the family. When they are told to "play quietly because Mommy is resting," and they later are told that "Mommy is worse," children may conclude that they did not play quietly enough.

Parents may not be able to attend non-essential social functions with the child, such as to assist as "class-room mothers" for school parties, attend soccer games, or church musical productions. Children may feel alone, resentful of the needs of the ill parent, and abandoned.

Children may be expected to assume additional responsibilities at home in care-giving roles with the ill parent. When children are included in working together with the family to meet the needs of the chronically ill parent, they feel valued and needed. When they are asked to relinquish too much of their childhood, they feel sad.

What **YOU** Can Do to Help the Child Who Lives With a Chronically Ill Parent

1. Give focused, one-to-one attention in brief time spurts. Five minutes of focused attention is more valuable than fifty minutes of general attention.

2. Demonstrate active interest in school and church activities that are important to the child. Ask specific questions to show you remember what the child has already told you.

3. Tell the child when and where he can make noise, run, and play. If space is limited, give the ill parent ear plugs.

4. Thank the child for the help he provides, but do not communicate that the child's value is related only to helping the sick parent. The child who assumes a care giver identity will sacrifice his childhood.

5. Write notes or make phone calls to the school teacher to communicate changes in the status of the sick family member, so the teacher can understand the child's behavior.

6. Limit the number of care givers that provide baby-sitting during hospitalizations, or other times the healthy parent is unable to provide care. Find care givers that are nurturing, playful, sensitive, and liked by the child.

7. Avoid spoiling the child out of guilt. Children who live with a chronically ill parent can grow up as caring, kind, responsible adults, but they must have structure and limits.

8. Encourage the ill parent to be involved with the child in whatever way is possible. Showing interest in school art, listening to the child practice the piano, smiles, and expressing love and gratitude are all helpful.

9. Maintain a sense of humor

Conversation Starters

"I notice that it is hard for you to go outside and play when Mommy is especially sick. Do you think we expect you to stay inside to help?"

"Would you like me to explain the disease that has made Daddy sick?"

"Tell me all about what happened at school today. I have time now that is just for you."

"Sometimes kids feel guilty when they have a sick parent. But kids can't make a parent sick even if they make noise or are naughty. What else are you worried about?"

"What do you worry about?"

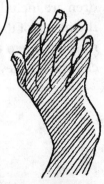

Pointing the Child to God

Children need to know that God hears their prayers, whether or not He chooses to heal their parent. God will give them the courage to take a day at a time.

WHY IS DADDY SICK ALL THE TIME?

Why Is This So Hard?

Maybe your parent has been sick for such a long time, you can't remember a time before the illness. Getting used to the illness doesn't mean that it is easier though. Maybe you don't know any other kids who have a parent who is always sick, and none of your friends really understands. That would be very hard. Maybe you even get mad at your parent for being sick, sometimes. You know that doesn't make sense because, of course, they don't want to be sick, but it is how you feel!

How Do Other Kids Feel?

Most kids worry when they have a parent who is sick. Sometimes they have a hard time understanding what is really wrong with the parent, and sometimes kids hear adult conversations that they don't understand about what the doctor said. Most kids worry that their parent might die, and that would be the worst thing of all!

Usually kids feel sad that their sick parent is not able to go camping or play ball or go to the beach. Kids are confused about why God doesn't just make their parent better when they have prayed that He would. Trusting God when we don't understand what He is doing is hard!

Kids feel guilty because they think they did something to make their parent sick, but of course, they didn't.

This is how I feel

_____

_____

_____

_____

I Can Help Myself

1. If my parent needs an organ transplant, I can pray for a perfect match donor to be available. And, I can pray for the family of the donor.
2. I can ask my sick parent what they have learned about God because of the illness.
3. I can ask my sick parent to tape record stories that happened when they were little, so I can listen to their voice anytime I want.
4. I can play hard, enjoy my friends, and remember that even though my parent is ill, they want me to have fun.

I Can Make Good Choices

1. I can talk about my feelings, all of them, even the bad feelings like worry, fear, anger, resentment, or sadness.
2. I can ask my parents what my job is in helping the family. When I am done with my job, I can go and play.
3. I can ask the school counselor if there are other children who have a parent who is chronically sick, and ask her if we could all talk together.
4. I can ask my Sunday school teacher to tell me a story about how Jesus responded to a person with a chronic illness.

I Can Trust God to Be There for Me

Bible Verse: "For I am the Lord, your God, who takes hold of your right hand and says to you, Do not fear; I will help you" (Isaiah 41:13).

Prayer: Dear God, I am so glad that in heaven nobody will ever be sick again. Thank you for being close and helping our family right now. Help me to trust you with all my fears. Amen.

The child with a
CRITICALLY ILL PARENT

Understanding the Child

Children and adults may experience shock and emotional numbness with a sudden, unexpected tragic accident or illness in a parent. The younger the child the more vulnerable he is to separation from his source of security.

When one parent is critically ill, the other parent is also unavailable to the child since he is probably spending most of his time at the hospital. Children feel best when they are included, not shut out from the family events, even the painful events.

During a critical illness children are frequently sent to stay with relatives or other care-givers, where there will be different house rules, possible separation from loved siblings, pets, and familiar routine. All of these changes result in feelings of loss.

Children sense the seriousness of the situation whether or not they are specifically told about it. Since their security is directly linked to the well-being of their parent, an emotionally distraught parent evokes deep fear. Children at approximately six years and older KNOW that their parent might die from a serious injury or illness.

When children visit the critically ill parent at the hospital, there are frequently other sources of fear such as, the parent may be unconscious; there may be multiple tubes and machines going into the parent's body; there will be many doctors and nurses, and there may be visible blood. Care-givers are usually too busy to provide the thorough, simple explanation that children need to feel safe in a critical care environment.

What YOU Can Do to Help the Child With a Critically Ill Parent

1. Don't lie about the seriousness of the parent's illness. Say, "Your Daddy is very sick, but the doctor is working hard to help him."

2. Tell the truth. Say, "I don't know," to questions about why this tragedy happened, and then add, "God is here with us and He will help us".

3. Touch, hold, hug to provide comfort and support.

4. Explain the purpose of the equipment in the hospital room in simple language. If you don't know, ask the nurse and then rephrase it for the child.

5. Don't talk too much. Tell the child that he can ask anything he chooses and that you will always tell the truth. Let the child be in charge of what he wants to know.

6. Talk to the child about his weekly routine and give him permission to do normal things. "Your soccer game is on Saturday and Uncle Bill will take you. It is okay to play soccer even though your mommy is very sick."

7. Don't promise that the parent will be just fine, because children will feel additionally betrayed if a parent dies or has long term complications.

8. Children rarely can put all of their feelings into words. They usually express how they really feel in the way they behave. Frightened children often regress and act in less mature ways.

9. Maintain the normal daily routine and rules as much as possible. Children feel secure when they are expected to obey and are not allowed to act out of control.

10. Give children additional opportunity for vigorous physical play which allows their anger to be expressed in an appropriate way.

11. Help children feel needed by teaching them some helpful activity to assist the ill parent, such as making a picture for the hospital room, picking flowers, etc.

Conversation Starters

"Do you want to go to the hospital with me to see your mommy, or would you rather stay home with the others this time? You are in charge of deciding."

"Tell me about what happened to your daddy."

"Whatever you would like to know, please ask me. I will tell you the truth."

"Both your mommy and daddy are having a hard time right now. You are safe here and we will take good care of you. Is there a special toy you would like to get from home?"

"Would you like me to read this story about another little girl who had a very sick parent?"

Pointing the Child to God

Children need to know that God sees their heart even when they can't put their feelings into words.

MY MOM IS SO SICK I'M SCARED

Why Does This Hurt So Much?

One of the reasons that having a very sick parent is so hard for kids is that adults might not know that you have lots of questions and that you want to be told what is happening. You can tell them what you need.

Kids handle problems in the way that is right for them, so how you feel is probably different from how your sister feels. Everybody handles feelings in their own way.

How Do Other Kids Feel?

Kids feel scared when their mom or dad is very, very ill. There are so many new and hard experiences, like having someone else take care of you while the grown-ups are at the hospital, and questions that you want to ask, such as, "What will happen next?"

Lots of kids wonder if they did something that caused their parent to be so sick, but kids can never make their mom or dad ill. It is just something that happens.

Kids don't know what to say when other kids ask them questions. Sometimes kids with a very sick parent don't like to talk about it. It is okay to decide who and when you want to talk about what is happening. Usually when kids ask questions about the things they worry about, they feel better.

This is how I feel

_____

_____

_____

_____

I Can Help Myself

1. I can ask to keep something that belongs to my sick parent, such as a necklace or my daddy's T-shirt to sleep in. This will help me feel close to my sick parent.
2. I can ask questions about the things that I wonder about, such as, "What is a heart attack, anyway?"
3. I can play and have fun. It doesn't mean that I'm not worried or that I don't care about what is happening.
4. I can cry if I want to.

I Can Make Good Choices

1. I will be patient with myself and my brothers and sisters. Everybody is upset right now. It's normal to be upset.
2. I can choose to believe the grown-ups when they tell me that nothing I did made this happen.
3. I can tell my school teacher and Sunday school teacher about what happened. They will want to help me.
4. I can ask to visit my sick parent and sit close and pray.

I Can Trust God to Be There for Me

Bible Verse: "God is our refuge and strength, an ever-present help in trouble" (Psalm 46:1).

Prayer: Dear God, I've never been this scared before. Thank you for telling us to pray when someone is sick. My parent needs you. I need you, too. Amen.

The child exposed to

CULTS

Understanding the Child

Young children lack the sophisticated skills to know right and wrong religious beliefs. They are in the gradual process of understanding the teaching of their own church.

Children believe that if an adult said it, it must be true. Initially, what happens at church and how they are treated is more important to children than content of what is taught.

By the time children are in Junior High School, they may make decisions about cult affiliation due to peer relationships or emotional need to belong to a group. Much recruiting occurs by cults seeking to entice Junior High and High School youth into membership. Approximately 50% of High School students state that they have been approached by a cult member.

Children join cults because they have needs that are not being met elsewhere, because they are seeking a strong leader who will tell them what to do, because the cult claims to offer solutions to their own personal problems, or, the cult suggests ways to make the world a more loving place. The idealism of adolescents makes them vulnerable to the promise of a better world for all humanity. Teenagers may also join cults as an act of rebellion against their parents.

Since cults focus on their similarities to Christian belief, rather than differences, children may initially see the cult as offering the same teaching as their original home church.

Teenagers who join cults are most likely to come from suburban, middle-class families.

What YOU Can Do to Help the Child Exposed to Cults

1. Children need to be told that different churches worship God in different ways, and that some churches emphasize certain beliefs more than others. This difference in the way people worship is not wrong.

2. Children can understand that although the style of worship may be different, there are basic Christian beliefs that are not negotiable. For example, to be called a Christian, a person must believe that Jesus Christ is the only true God.

3. Children need to know the names of some of the cults that are most active in their local community.

4. Children can be told that cults often have common characteristics, such as:

   a. A strong living leader who controls the group and is treated by the members as if he or she is divine.

   b. They recruit members in sneaky ways, such as saying that they are a nondenominational Bible study group.

   c. Cults teach that they have all of the answers and everything is right or wrong without any gray areas.

   d. They exercise control over members who have less and less freedom as the cult takes over most of the decisions of their lives.

5. Children who are thoroughly nurtured, enjoyed, valued at home will be less vulnerable to the attraction of joining a cult.

6. Adults can show courtesy and respect for cult members who come to their houses, become informed about the cult's teaching so that they can present the teaching of the Bible in discussions with cult members, and pray for those in cults.

Conversation Starters

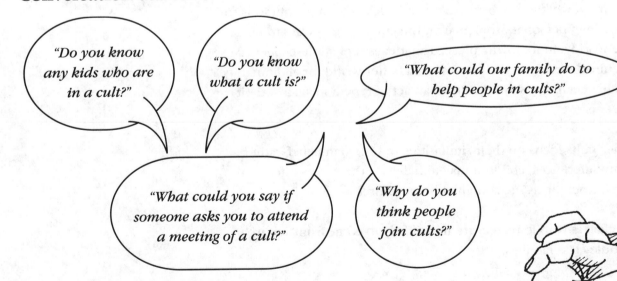

"Do you know any kids who are in a cult?"

"Do you know what a cult is?"

"What could our family do to help people in cults?"

"What could you say if someone asks you to attend a meeting of a cult?"

"Why do you think people join cults?"

Pointing the Child to God

Children need to know at least one Bible verse that states that Jesus Christ is God, and that the Bible is the source of direction for the Christian life.

WHAT DO YOU KNOW ABOUT CULTS?

What Is a Cult?

A cult is a false religious group. Sometimes cults use some of the same words that you have heard at church, but usually the words mean something different to a person in a cult. Cults teach that they know all of the truth.

A Cult Is Wrong

A cult believes things that are not true. A cult also behaves in a way that hurts people. For example, a cult discourages a person from thinking for himself. Cults usually have a very strong leader who tells people what to believe and what to do. Cults have strong rules that control people, and usually people in cults are taught that they have to do lots of good works to be accepted by the cult.

Why Would Anyone Join a Cult?

Some people join cults because their parents were members, and others join because they want someone to tell them what to believe and what to do, and some people join because they think that the cult can make the world a better place for everyone to live. And some people join the cult because the cult teaches that the wrong things they want to do are not sinful, so they don't need to feel guilty.

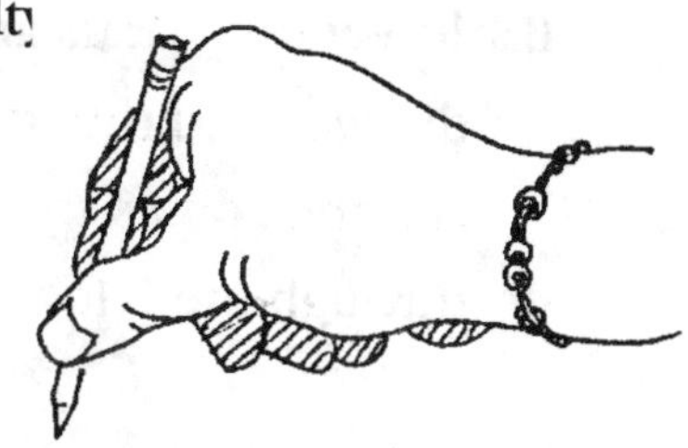

This is how I feel

_____

_____

_____

_____

I Can Help Myself

1. If I have a friend who is in a cult, I can learn what that cult believes by asking my parents, checking a book out of the church library, or asking my Sunday school teacher.
2. If I don't understand how being a Christian is different from being a cult member, I will ask someone who can explain it simply.
3. I can look for ways to talk to my friend about Jesus and share the Bible verses that I have learned.
4. I can love kids who aren't Christians. I can be a light for Jesus.
5. I can spend time with people who are Christians and who encourage me to live like a Christian.

I Can Trust God to Be There for Me

Bible Verse: "Jesus answered, "I am the way and the truth and the life. No one comes to the Father except through me" (John 14:6).

Prayer: Dear God, thank you for telling us the good news about Jesus so clearly that even kids can understand. Amen.

I Can Make Good Choices

1. I won't get into arguments about the cult being wrong. I will just say what I have learned in the Bible.
2. I will pray for people in cults.
3. I will read my Bible so I know the truth.
4. I will remember that cults make people feel good, but feeling good is not the same thing as being right about something.

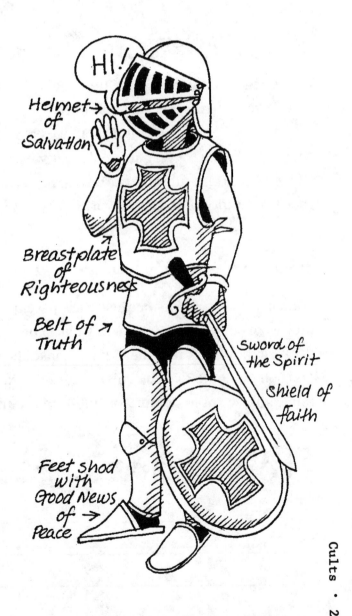

HI!

Helmet of Salvation

Breastplate of Righteousness

Belt of Truth

Sword of the Spirit

Shield of Faith

Feet shod with Good News of Peace

The child who is grieving a
DEATH

Understanding the Child

When a death occurs in the family, adults may be preoccupied with their own feelings of grief and be unable to support the children. Children of all ages grieve, including infants. The younger the child the longer the grief lasts.

Because children grieve in ways unique to child-hood, their grief work may not be recognized by adults. Children are not short adults. They grieve through their behavior and in their play, not by talking about their feelings. What a child is doing is how he feels. Grieving children may act out in anger toward siblings, be especially clinging, com-plain of tummy aches, or withdraw. Grief fits the child.

Children may hurt themselves out of feelings of guilt and the desire to be punished for making Daddy die. This guilt results from the normal belief of young children that they are the cause of all that happens in the world.

Since children cannot tolerate intensely painful feelings for long periods, they grieve in spurts; that is, they may cry or talk about their sad feelings, and then minutes later go out to play in a casual way. The child simply needs a breather from the emotional pain.

Young children grieve the death at each developmental stage. A three year old cannot know what it means to grow up without a mommy, and will grieve again the loss through all stages of growth as the meaning becomes more and more clear.

What YOU Can Do to Help the Grieving Child

1. Provide focused one-to-one attention in playing with the child. Let the child be the leader in the play.
2. Assume that the child is grieving in the right way. Don't try to get a child to talk about it. Children will express their feelings in the way that is comfortable for them.
3. Don't try to soften the experience by using fancy language. Use plain and simple words. Daddy didn't pass away, he died.
4. Recognize the child's searching for the person who died. It is impossible for young children to comprehend that a person is gone forever until they are about nine or ten years old.
5. Grieving adults and children often develop fantasies of sainthood about the dead family member. This is normal and will be given up when the child no longer needs to do it.
6. Don't say, "Now you're the man of the house." Children need permission to be children and to be cared for.
7. In talking with children, don't put all of the focus on Heaven and none on the feelings of loss.
8. Don't pressure or encourage children to cry. Children need permission to cry or not to cry. Grief is not measured by tears.
9. Don't send children away to baby-sitters to protect them from the family sadness. Include them. Let them decide when they want to go out to play or want to be with the adults.
10. Don't promise you won't die. Say, "I think I will live until I am very, very old, but no one knows for sure when they will die.
11. Don't single a child out for special privileges. Maintain the same rules and routine as before the death. It helps children feel safe.

Conversation Starters

"Would you like me to read what the Bible says about Heaven?"

"I'd like to tell you about the funeral and then you can ask any questions you want before you decide if you want to go."

"What should grown-ups know about how children feel after a death?"

"When you are scared, just squeeze my hand. I will stop what I am doing and hold you until you feel okay."

"I know that you miss your baby brother. What is the hardest part about all of this for you?"

"Would you like me to explain what made Grandpa die?"

Pointing the Child to God

Children need to know that Jesus cried when his friend, Lazarus, died, and that they don't have to be brave and strong.

WHY DO PEOPLE HAVE TO DIE?

Why Does This Hurt So Much?

Even if you knew that the death was coming, it is still a very big shock when someone you love dies. Probably nothing this bad has ever happened to you before and you don't know what to do. Sometimes grown-ups say that everything will be just fine, or that they are happy that the person is in Heaven, but you know they also have sad feelings because they are crying. It is very confusing.

It is also a scary time. You don't know what to expect next, your schedule changes, and the adults in your family are upset. Who wouldn't be scared!

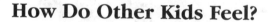

How Do Other Kids Feel?

Most kids say that when someone in the family dies, it is the worst thing that has ever happened to them, and that they feel very, very badly about it.

Maybe there isn't another kid in your classroom or neighborhood who has had someone they love die, and you don't know how other kids feel.

It is normal to feel angry at times, but some kids wonder if their angry thoughts made the person die. Feeling angry never makes a person die.

Kids also wonder who will take care of them if their parents die. It helps to ask your parents because they probably know who it would be.

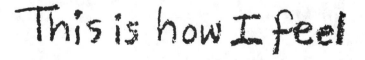

This is how I feel

_____

_____

_____

_____

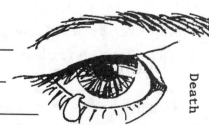

I Can Help Myself

1. I can ask to keep a special reminder of the person who died, like a favorite book or collection.
2. I can tell grown-ups if I want to go to the cemetery or funeral home where I can ask questions.
3. I can get my feelings out by playing hard outside or by doing art work to show how I feel.
4. I can look through the picture albums and remember the special times I had with the person.

I Can Make Good Choices

1. I can read children's books about other kids who have had a death of a loved person.
2. I can tell my parents that I need a hug or a night light for awhile. I know I won't always feel like this.
3. I can ask what made the person die.
4. I can write a letter to someone else who feels very sad about the death, and tell them why I loved the person who died.

I Can Trust God to Be There for Me

Bible Verse: "Even though I walk through the valley of the shadow of death, I will fear no evil, for you are with me" (Psalm 23:4).

Prayer: Dear God, death is so scary and sad. I'm glad that you promised that in Heaven there won't be any more death. Amen.

The child who lives with a
DEPRESSED ADULT

Understanding the Child

Parents may be unavailable to children because of their physical or emotional absence. Children experience grief when they are deprived of nurture and parenting for whatever reason it may occur.

Symptoms of depression in adults include: feeling inadequate, helpless and hopeless, withdrawing from friends and activities, difficulty sleeping, loss of appetite, and constant tiredness.

Children may misinterpret the symptoms which commonly accompany depression as indicators of their own lack of worthiness for the one-to-one attention they crave. For example, the parent who is chronically fatigued, and experiences little joy in life will have minimal enthusiasm to play with children. Children cannot understand that the disease of depression has caused their parent's lack of interest in them.

Children view life in simplistic terms. A person is sick when they are injured, or coughing, or throwing up. It is difficult for them to comprehend an illness that affects feelings. Children are likely to think that a parent just doesn't want to parent them, when actually the parent is emotionally unable to do so.

The depressed parent is often irritable and has less tolerance for misbehavior, or normal noisy play, so children are more frequently in trouble.

The depressed adult who worries constantly may communicate that the world is not a safe place.

What YOU Can Do to Help the Child Who Lives With a Depressed Person

1. Children need to be told that depression is an illness, like other illnesses, and that it can be treated. The person can get better. Showing children information in a health book may establish this credibility.

2. Children are helped by reviewing the symptoms of the parent's illness. Say, "Your dad doesn't always feel like playing football with you because he has the disease of depression." He won't always feel like this.

3. Be clear that the parent is not choosing to be depressed, and that the depressed parent wants the sad feelings to go away as much as the child.

4. Provide additional nurture for children who live with a depressed parent by hugs, smiles, pats, and verbal praise.

5. Provide physical space that encourages children to play hard, be noisy, silly, and giggle.

6. Build the child's self esteem by honest affirmation which relates to being a child, i.e. don't praise the child for taking good care of the parent.

7. Encourage children to talk about their own feelings, even the bad feelings, with the depressed parent. Say, "It is okay to tell your mom that you feel sad when she doesn't come to watch your piano recital."

8. Children who live with a depressed parent are often frightened. They know they need a parent who takes care of them. Offer yourself in specific ways.

9. Children are anxious when a depressed adult threatens suicide and they may feel responsible to prevent such an act. Tell children that only adults take care of adults.

10. Minimize the child's guilt by saying that children never have the power to make an adult get depressed.

11. Children who have a depressed parent may have difficulty concentrating at school and need additional support with homework.

Conversation Starters

"Sometimes kids have problems that are hard to talk about. If that is true for you, please remember that I really want to help you."

"I like being with you. Could you use some help with your homework?"

"Would you like to hear some of the things I especially like about you?"

"Tell me what you know about the disease of depression."

Pointing the Child to God

Children need to know that God cares about how we feel as well as what we do.

WHAT IS DEPRESSION?

Why Is This So Hard?

If you are living with a depressed adult, you might be feeling confused, and lonely, and worried. It is hard to understand that an adult can have a disease that makes them feel sad, and tired, and irritable, but it happens. Lots of adults have the disease of depression and need a doctor to help them. Usually depressed adults take medicine to make them feel less sad, and they usually need to talk to a counselor to learn other ways of taking care of themselves, such as talking to friends about their feelings and taking walks.

Sometimes depressed adults feel so badly that they try to hurt themselves. If that happens, they might have to go to a special hospital called a psychiatric hospital for awhile. You might wonder if you caused the adult to get depressed because of the kind of kid you are. The answer is that there is nothing that kids can do to make their parents depressed.

How Do Other Kids Feel?

Kids wish the depressed adult had the energy to come and watch them play soccer or be in the school play. They feel badly because the depressed adult is quiet and doesn't talk to them or help them at home as much. It is scary if the depressed adult tries to hurt themselves. Most kids don't like the extra responsibility they have at home while their parent is depressed. Kids know they need to help with chores, but they want the adults to do the adult jobs, like cook meals and take care of the baby.

This is how I feel

_____

_____

_____

_____

I Can Help Myself

1. I can ask questions about the medications given for depression, and psychologists, and what is done to help depression.
2. I can take walks with the depressed adult because it is good for them and gives me time alone with the adult.
3. I can believe it when adults tell me that kids never cause an adult to have the disease of depression.
4. I can ask for help and hugs. I don't have to be brave all of the time.

I Can Make Good Choices

1. I can spend time with caring adults who are not depressed.
2. I can ask my school counselor about ways to take care of myself while the adult in my home is depressed.
3. I can spend time every day playing hard, talking about my real feelings, and remembering that although this might last one or two years, it won't last forever.
4. I can write a report about depression for school. It would give me a chance to learn more about it.

I Can Trust God to Be There for Me

Bible Verse: "Trust in the Lord with all your heart and lean not on your own understanding; in all your ways acknowledge him, and he will make your paths straight" (Proverbs 3:5,6).

Prayer: Dear God, I am so glad that you are with me, even when you feel far away, and that the Bible is true. Our family needs your help right now. Amen.

The child experiencing
DIVORCE

Understanding the Child

Children respond to divorce differently than their parents, and therefore the impact of divorce on children may Lbe minimized. Children often remain faithful to their biological parents, even when a happy remarriage occurs.

Children of divorce often feel grief and shame and embarrassment. They feel that in some way they have caused their parents to divorce. Since children measure love by physical distance, when one parent leaves the home, children assume that it is because the parent does not love them enough to stay. Children lack awareness of the amount of effort that parents may have invested in attempting to resolve their difficulties.

Boys usually appear more stressed than girls at the time of the divorce, but both boys and girls commonly show long range "fall out" that may not be apparent until late adolescence.

Lowered self-esteem and difficulty in concentrating will often be apparent in poor school grades. Other common responses to divorce include difficulty in getting along with other children, fear that the custodial parent will also leave, and, worry that the family will not have enough money.

Children feel angry because they believe that if their parents had tried a little harder the divorce would not have occurred. They also believe that the divorce would not hurt so much if they had been just a little older or a little younger when the divorce happened.

What **YOU** Can Do to Help the Child

1. Don't criticize or blame the other parent for the divorce.
2. Tell the child that their parents have really tried to work out the problems without disclosing details.
3. Don't give children false hope that the marriage can be fixed.
4. Tell children they didn't cause the divorce and they can't bring their parents back together.
5. Tell children how often they will visit the non custodial parent and adhere rigidly to the visiting schedule the first year until trust is established.
6. Give a little information at a time and then invite children to ask questions. If they ask private details, tell them that particular information is just between the parents.
7. Read stories about other children whose parents divorced.
8. Give information about the divorce to all the children in the family at the same time.
9. Allow children to feel sad, even if the parents feel relief. Don't tell children to be strong and brave.
10. Children need permission to take time out from the stress to play and have fun. Young children express their feelings in play, not words.
11. Maintain the same rules about chores, homework and bedtime, as before the divorce. It helps children feel safe.
12. Keep a positive attitude. Children can and do heal. They are not permanent victims of a broken home.

Conversation Starters

"It is okay with me for you to talk to your friends about the divorce if you want to tell them how you are feeling. You have a right to get all the support you need."

"Usually children have questions about a divorce. Is there anything you wonder about?"

"Can you name one thing we could do that would make this hard time a little easier for you?"

"What is the hardest part about this divorce for you?"

"I know that you still love your daddy. You can tell the truth about how you feel. You don't have to hide your feelings to protect me."

Pointing the Child to God

Children need to know that God, their heavenly Father, will never leave them, and that God loves their mom and dad.

MY PARENTS ARE GETTING A DIVORCE

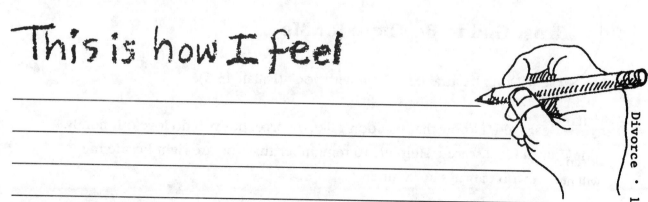

Why Does This Hurt So Much?

Divorce is a big change in your family, so you probably have lots of feelings about what is happening.

Sometimes adults don't know how worried or upset kids feel, so it helps to talk about how you feel. Bad feelings that are talked about, don't seem quite so bad anymore.

Some kids wonder if they still have a real family after a divorce. The answer is yes even when their mom and dad don't live in the same house.

How Do Other Kids Feel?

Some kids say that during the divorce they feel sad, mad, lonely, and worried. Children also say that they feel happy that some of the fighting between their parents has stopped, and that sometimes Dad spends more time with them now than before the divorce. Some kids say that it is fun to have two houses to live in, and that they hate it when their mom or dad starts dating someone else. Some kids say they wish their parent would talk to other adults instead of telling kids their problems. Kids have lots of different feelings. Whatever you are feeling is right for you.

This is how I feel

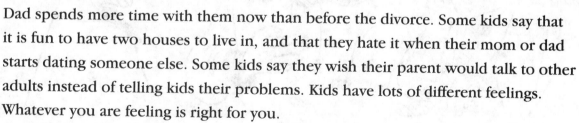

_____

_____

_____

_____

I Can Help Myself

1. Asking my mom and dad if there is anything I did to make the divorce happen. If they say "no," believe them!
2. Asking questions over again when I don't understand.
3. Telling my mom and dad when I need a hug.
4. Asking my friends how they felt when their parents got a divorce and what helped them feel better.
5. Leaving the room if my parents fight and turning the radio on or going outside to play.

I Can Make Good Choices

1. I can ask for what I need, such as asking for a drawer, or a box of my own where I can put my things when I visit my non custodial parent.
2. I can kick a ball to get my mad feelings out, so that I don't take my feelings out on my little brother.
3. I can show good manners to my dad's new girlfriend.
4. I can ask to talk to my grandpa on the phone, if I don't get to visit him after the divorce.
5. I can talk to God about my feelings.

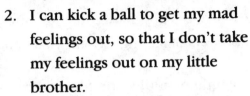

I Can Trust God to Be There for Me

Bible Verse: "Don't be afraid, for I am with you" (Isaiah 43:5).

Prayer: Dear God, I know that you don't like divorce, but you do love our family. Sometimes I feel scared. Help me to remember that you are right beside me, and that I won't always hurt. Amen.

The child concerned about
DRUG ABUSE

Understanding the Child

Children are usually exposed to drug abuse in grade school. Information about how to resist an offer of drugs, what an illicit drug is and why it is illegal, what an illegal drug looks like, and what harm it will do, should all be taught to children by the time they are in the third grade.

Children who live with a drug abusing parent may experience much neglect because addicts place a higher priority on acquiring and using drugs than nurturing and caring for children. Living with a parent who abuses drugs is a form of emotional abandonment with devastating impact. Children need surrogate parenting from other caring adults.

Children tend to have simplistic answers to complex problems, so understanding the idea of psychological and emotional dependence on drugs is difficult for children to understand. Why doesn't the parent just stop using drugs?

Children experience long-term grief for the loss of the relationship with the parent who has chosen drug abuse. Children may follow the model of their parents by experimenting with drugs at an early age, or they may totally reject illegal chemicals.

Children may have been exposed to drugs before they were born if their parents used drugs. Children exposed to drugs during pregnancy often have learning difficulties and other neurological problems for the rest of their lives.

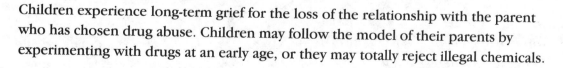

What YOU Can Do to Help the Child

1. Don't be afraid to set limits and be clear about expectations for the child's behavior. Children need structure to feel safe.
2. Teach children who live with a family member who abuses drugs what to do in an emergency, how to call the police, fire department, etc.
3. Tell children they may call you if they need a ride and you will take them to a safe place.
4. Teach children about addiction. Tell them addicts cannot stop without help.
5. Provide warm affection, fun, and avoid criticism of their drug abusing family member.
6. Contact drug treatment agencies to learn factual information about specific drugs .
7. Encourage activities that build a strong sense of self worth (sports, music, etc.). Children who feel good about themselves will be able to refuse drugs more easily.
8. Role play saying "no" to offers of drugs by peers.
9. Tell children what will happen if they experiment with drugs. Make the discipline specific and follow-through.
10. Learn the physical and behavioral signs of drug abuse, such as spending time with people who abuse drugs, unexplained need for money, changes in grooming, appetite, and sleep habits.
11. Tell children the difference between medicine and illegal drugs.
12. Read stories about other children who have lived with a drug abusing family member.
13. Provide family meetings once a week and require attendance by everyone in the family. Allow confrontation and freedom to express feelings about the drug abuse.

Conversation Starters

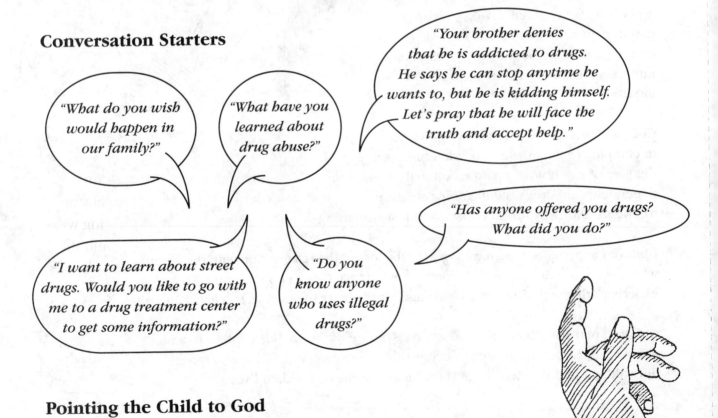

"What do you wish would happen in our family?"

"What have you learned about drug abuse?"

"Your brother denies that he is addicted to drugs. He says he can stop anytime he wants to, but he is kidding himself. Let's pray that he will face the truth and accept help."

"Has anyone offered you drugs? What did you do?"

"I want to learn about street drugs. Would you like to go with me to a drug treatment center to get some information?"

"Do you know anyone who uses illegal drugs?"

Pointing the Child to God

Children need to know that God only says no to things that hurt us. That includes drugs. He does this because He wants what is best for us.

YOU KNOW HOW BAD DRUGS CAN BE

Why Does This Hurt So Much?

Living with someone who abuses drugs can be very difficult, and you deserve help. You might feel that you are alone, but lots of other kids have the very same problem.

One thing you should know is that there are grown-ups who can help you. It is okay to tell a safe adult about what is happening at your home. This is not a secret you have to keep. Even if the person doesn't stop abusing drugs, you can learn to be happy and grow up to be a strong, good person, who never abuses drugs.

You are an expert on how much drugs can hurt a family, so you know why it is important to say no to drugs when they are offered to you.

How Do Other Kids Feel?

Kids feel sad because a family member who abuses drugs usually has other things to think about besides kids interests. Kids feel angry because the abuser doesn't stop using drugs even when they know that the drugs hurt them. And they feel lonely because when drugs are abused, the grown-ups are usually not much fun to live with. Lots of kids say that the family fights are the worst part of living with an addict. Kids are embarrassed because they know drug abuse is against the law, and they don't want anybody to know about the problem in their family.

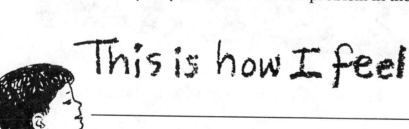

This is how I feel

_____

_____

_____

_____

I Can Help Myself

1. I can cry when I feel sad. I don't have to pretend drugs aren't a problem at my house.
2. I can spend time with kind grown-ups, like my Sunday school teacher or my best friend's parents.
3. I can write down all of the reasons why using drugs is a dumb thing to do.
4. I can learn about other ways to get a high, such as running or getting involved in a hobby that is fun.
5. I can practice saying "no" to drugs very loudly into my tape recorder.

I Can Make Good Choices

1. I can read about drugs so I know what drugs do to people.
2. I can stay away from places where drugs are used, and I can remember to never pick up a syringe or needle from the ground.
3. I can listen to music with words that make me love Jesus.
4. I can decide to avoid using drugs and choose friends who don't want to use drugs.
5. I can love the person who abuses drugs but not his behavior.

I Can Trust God to Be There for Me

Bible Verse: "God is faithful; he will not let you be tempted beyond what you can bear" (1 Corinthians 10:13).

Prayer: Dear God, please help the person I love to stop using drugs, and help me to grow up to be strong and to serve you with my mind, my heart, and my body. Amen.

The child with an

EATING DISORDER

Understanding the Child

Children grow up exposed to a constant media blitz which equates small body size to self worth. "If you are thin you will be popular, beautiful, desirable." One-half of all girls go on a self-imposed diet during their teen-age years. In addition, many children will be in families with a parent who is frequently dieting and reinforcing the value of being thin.

Children learn that food is not only a way to comfort and nurture themselves emotionally, but it is also a powerful weapon controlling their parents. What, and how much a child eats will merit the parent's attention.

Children who have experienced abuse or neglect in their early years, frequently horde or eat large amounts of food, which is a pattern unrelated to the child's hunger. These children are usually not overweight, although they may eat as much as an adult. At times they will eat until they vomit, attempting to satisfy a hunger that cannot be filled by food.

The eating disorders of anorexia (deliberate starvation) and bulimia (overeating which is followed by purging) are medically life-threatening disorders and cannot be managed by parents. Medical and psychological expertise is mandatory, since these children may die without treatment.

Anorexia and bulimia are disorders that almost exclusively affect girls. One out of every ten girls over twelve years of age has struggled with either anorexia or bulimia. Girls who have not had an eating disorder will likely know someone who has. Girls in Junior High School are especially vulnerable to eating disorders.

What YOU Can Do to Help the Child With an Eating Disorder

1. Be cautious about purchasing dolls that reinforce the myth that being tall and skinny makes a person valuable.
2. Provide models of women who enjoy life, feel good about themselves, and are not thin. 60% of all models and ballerinas have eating disorders.
3. Get factual information about eating disorders in order to respond in helpful ways, i.e. recognize that anorexia is not a loss of appetite but deliberate control of how much and what food is eaten.
4. Utilize every possible means of showing unconditional acceptance of the child just as she is; acceptance that is not based on physical appearance, talent, or intellect.
5. Respond to failure in a casual manner. Girls with eating disorders often feel that their parents expect a great deal from them and they cannot live up to these expectations.
6. Give children the freedom to make choices and exercise control appropriate to the child's age, without pressure to succeed. Share your own failures and poor choices in growing up.
7. Be aware of weight loss that may be camouflaged by loose fitting clothing, lies about having eaten somewhere else prior to a meal at home, or by eating normally followed by vomiting in the toilet after the meal or using diuretics or laxatives.
8. Don't try to use reason to convince an anorexic child that she is too thin. These children feel fat no matter what the mirror or the bathroom scale indicates.
9. Anorexia children may choose to be excessively involved in food preparation at home. Discourage the child's help in the kitchen, or looking at magazines about food, reading recipes, or in talking about food.

Conversation Starters

"Your Dad and I will support whatever decision you make about going with your friend's parents to the beach. Do whatever you want. What are some of your concerns about going?"

"We are not going to require that you eat in front of us or that you promise to gain weight. We know that we can't control your eating. We are just going to love you and let the doctor help you with your eating problem."

"I know that you didn't win, but did you have fun?"

"I think that your periods have stopped because you have lost so much weight. I've made a doctor's appointment for you. I'll wait in the waiting room while you and the doctor talk privately."

Pointing the Child to God

Children need to know that God asks us to glorify Him in our bodies, but that He never asks us to do anything He won't help us do.

SOMETIMES EVEN EATING IS A PROBLEM

Why Does This Hurt So Much?

There are lots of reasons why you might be having an eating problem. If you are like most kids, you don't know why you have a problem with food or how you can stop behaviors that hurt you. When you watch TV, you might get the idea that other people will like you more if you are thin. Being self-conscious about your body is a really common problem. Kids who have an eating problem always need the help of a doctor. It isn't a problem that you can stop all by yourself. It is okay to ask for help. You deserve it!

How Do Other Kids Feel?

About half of the girls in your Junior High are concerned about their weight. They think they weigh too much. Some of them do weigh more than they should, and some of them think they are overweight when they really are too thin. Kids don't always see themselves like others see them.

Some girls have an eating problem called anorexia, which means that they starve themselves on purpose in order to lose weight. It is so serious that a girl might die from anorexia. Other girls have bulimia, which means that girls eat a lot of food in a big hurry and then make themselves vomit, or they take water pills or laxatives to lose the weight. Girls with bulimia aren't usually skinny. Both problems are serious. About one-fourth of girls with anorexia also develop bulimia.

This is how I feel

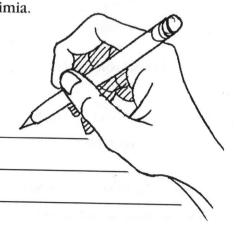

_____

_____

_____

_____

I Can Help Myself

1. I can talk about my angry, worried, scared feelings, as well as the good ones.
2. I can stop worrying about whether my parents are satisfied with me and just accept the love they offer.
3. I can read stories about other kids with eating problems.
4. I won't weigh myself every day, and I won't lie about whether I have eaten when my parents ask.

I Can Make Good Choices

1. I can accept the help that the therapist and doctor offer me but remember that I am the only one who can change my behavior.
2. I can spend time with warm, kind, accepting friends who will listen when I want to talk about my fears and problems.
3. I can spend more time with people and playing and less time alone thinking about food, my weight, and what people think about me.
4. I can write my feelings in a journal.
5. I can plan ways to reduce my stress when a difficult time is coming because I know I will have more trouble with food then.

I Can Trust God to Be There for Me

Bible Verse: "In all these things we are more than conquerors through him who loved us" (Romans 8:37).

Prayer: Dear God, I have problems I can't solve by myself. I need you in my life. Please help me now. Amen.

The **EMOTIONALLY ABUSED** child

Understanding the Child

Emotional abuse is controlling the child's behavior by rejection, humiliation, guilt, fear, teasing, demeaning remarks, or impossible standards. Emotionally abusive discipline is inconsistent, unpredictable, and excessive for the wrongdoing.

Emotional abuse is invisible abuse that leaves internal scars. The damage caused by emotional abuse may be more related to who did it than what exactly was done to the child. Children believe the assessments of their parents and verbal comments which embarrass, degrade, or reduce a child's sense of worth are abusive. Even when factual information is given to the child to offset this verbal abuse, children accept the remarks of their parents as the real truth about their value, skills, potential in life.

Even severely abusive parents rarely want to hurt their children. Emotional abuse may result from lack of alternative parenting skills to correct the child's misbehavior; short frustration tolerance, unrealistic expectations of a child due to lack of understanding of normal growth and development; lack of motivation to change; need for the child to give emotional support to the parent, rather than vise versa; chronic family stress such as financial problems; and mistrust toward offers of help from those outside the family.

Children most likely to be abused include handicapped, irritable, hyperactive, children who are intellectually slower or brighter than their parents; children who need less sleep than their parents; or unwanted children.

Behaviors of emotionally abused children include: not crying when hurt; delayed development; seeking excessive attention, even from strangers; being clingy and fearful; constantly fighting; eating excessively; cruelty to weaker children or animals; not knowing how to play with others; not listening or concentrating; nightmares; and being withdrawn and sad.

What YOU Can Do to Help the Emotionally Abused Child

1. Avoid making any negative comments about the abusive adult. Focus on the child's feelings. Say, "That must have made you feel very sad," rather than, "He shouldn't have said that."
2. Give children self-esteem building experiences, such as art projects which can be done the way the child chooses.
3. Offer child care on a regular basis so that parents have respite and the child has the opportunity to be in a positive, affirming atmosphere with you.
4. Don't compare children in the home. One child may be the scapegoat and be emotionally abused, while other children are affirmed and supported.
5. Avoid embarrassing or threatening the abusive adult, i.e. "The next time you tell her she is stupid, I am going to report you to the authorities." Instead say, "You are really having a hard time. I know a good parenting class that teaches helpful ways to make kids behave. Shall we go together?"
6. Listen without judgment to parents. Leave phone numbers of agencies that can help them, such as Parents Anonymous, and crisis intervention hot line numbers. Say, "They will respect you for seeking help and for trying to be a good parent."
7. Teach parents what worked for you. "Since kids believe everything their parents say about them, I always tried to count to ten before I said anything that might hurt my child's feelings."
8. Suggest that the parent gets counseling for depression, if that seems appropriate.
9. Tell children that parents sometimes need help, but that does not mean they do not love them.

Conversation Starters

"I love being with you. What would you like to do while we are together today?"

"You said that you are ugly and stupid. Tell me where you got those ideas about yourself. I see you as able to learn and nice looking."

"You don't want to go home after school? Tell me about that."

"You look sad. Are you?"

Pointing the Child to God

Children need to know that God is always fair, trustworthy, and kind.

WHAT IS EMOTIONAL ABUSE?

Why Does This Hurt So Much?

Maybe you have had your feelings hurt repeatedly by unkind words from an adult. If an important adult in your life acts like he doesn't accept you, or spend enough time with you, or is frequently mad at you, you probably feel sad and alone. Maybe you try not to talk too much at home for fear of upsetting someone and making matters worse than they are. Maybe you have found some ways to comfort yourself, such as by going to your room, or spending more time with other adults who are kind to you. Being emotionally abused can hurt very much, and you deserve to be helped.

Kids who are emotionally abused sometimes feel unsure of themselves, have nightmares, are afraid, tense, and worried. They sometimes think that if they were a better child, their parent wouldn't be so upset with them, but emotional abuse is a problem that some adults have, and it is never the fault of the child.

Sometimes when parents yell at kids, those kids yell at others. Kids learn how to get along with others by watching the way they themselves are treated at home. But they can learn new ways of getting along.

Boys are usually physically and emotionally abused more than girls.

This is how I feel

_____

_____

_____

I Can Help Myself

1. If an adult says, "You are the problem in our family," I can ask another adult that I trust, if it is true.
2. I can look for kind, gentle adults to be my friends.
3. I can admit I am afraid sometimes. I don't have to act tough.
4. I can spend time doing things that make me feel good about myself, such as playing with my dog or on a sports team.

I Can Make Good Choices

1. I won't yell or hit others. I know that doesn't solve any problems. I'll learn to talk about problems instead.
2. I'll ask my parents questions instead of just worrying and wondering: "Are you going to get a divorce?" "Do you love me?" "Would you learn to stop fighting with each other?"
3. I won't pretend that nothing hurts, when I know that it does hurt.
4. I can tell my teacher that our family needs help. And even if my parents refuse help, I deserve to be helped.

I Can Trust God to Be There for Me

Bible Verse: "May the words of my mouth and the meditation of my heart be pleasing in your sight, O Lord, my Rock and my Redeemer" (Psalm 19:14).

Prayer: Dear God, I can tell you the truth about how I feel. Thank you for being kind to me even when I have done something wrong. Amen.

The child with questions about
EUTHANASIA

Understanding the Child

The idea that an adult may believe that it is good to cause the death of a person is difficult for the young child to understand.

Children can understand that there is nothing more that the doctors can do to make Grandpa better and if he stops breathing, there won't be any CPR (passive euthanasia). It is more difficult for a child to understand why a person would ask a doctor or another person to do something to cause a person to die (active euthanasia).

Young children believe that adults can do anything they choose to do, and therefore doctors have the power to make anyone better. To learn that doctors are sometimes helpless is frightening.

Children should understand that active euthanasia of people, even when they have incurable illness, is illegal in most of the United States, in addition to not being a Christian concept. Even though a person is terminally ill or in pain, God can give people the power to tolerate hard circumstances and even to learn important lessons. Only God decides when a person should die.

Children may hear fancy language used to describe active euthanasia, such as "mercy killing" or "death with dignity," but describing it in such terms still doesn't make it right.

Children can be told that suicide is taking one's own life, and euthanasia is taking the life of another person who wants to die but is unwilling or unable to do it themselves. Both suicide and active euthanasia are wrong.

What **YOU** Can Do to Help the Child

1. Define terms for the child:

    Passive euthanasia: doing nothing to prevent the death of a person who is dying by natural means, when it is clear that more treatment would not make the person better. This is legal as well as acceptable as a Christian.

    Active euthanasia: doing something that causes the death of a person, usually a person who has an incurable illness, by giving them an overdose of medication or putting a gun in their hand, etc. This is against the law and not acceptable to a Christian.

2. Explain why active euthanasia is wrong. Say, "It is wrong because God said that murder is wrong and euthanasia is murder."

3. Tell children that even helping someone else do something wrong is still wrong for us.

4. Tell children that doctors do not always know how long a terminally ill person will live.

5. Explain that there might be pressure on a person to choose active euthanasia so that they won't be a burden on the family, or spend too much of the family money on health care that won't make the person well.

6. It is helpful to read newspaper articles and watch TV programs about active euthanasia with the child and talk about why you believe euthanasia is wrong.

Conversation Starters

"Would you like some help finding some verses in the Bible that tell why we believe euthanasia is against God's law?"

"How does God help people who are going through a hard time?"

"Why do you think some people believe that active euthanasia is okay?"

"Have you talked about euthanasia at school?"

"Have you heard about physician assisted suicide?

"Our neighbors have decided to remove the breathing machine from their father in the hospital and allow him to die. It is a sad time for them. Can you think of some ways we can comfort and help the family?"

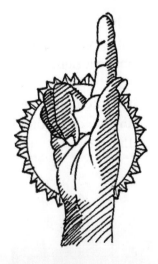

Pointing the Child to God

Children need to know that God values human life very much, including their own.

IT'S NEVER RIGHT TO MAKE SOMEONE DIE

Why Is This So Confusing?

You might hear some grown-ups talk about active euthanasia as if it is a kind and good thing to do. Adults might say that euthanasia is putting someone out of their misery, or ending their suffering, or mercy killing or death with dignity. These descriptions are used by people who want you to believe that making some one die is an acceptable thing to do, but it isn't.

People who believe in physician assisted suicide believe that a doctor should be allowed to give a person a drug that will make them die. They want the laws changed so that this will not be illegal. Even if it is legal, it would still be active euthanasia, the same thing as murder.

Sometimes an animal is suffering and a family takes it to the veterinarian to be put to sleep by an injection of a drug. Although this is a sad, hard time for the family, it is not the same as killing a person because people are made in God's image.

How Do Other Kids Feel?

Most kids want to have difficult topics explained in a clear way, so they understand why their parents and others they respect believe as they do. Kids like to be included when the family has discussions about what should be done if a parent becomes seriously hurt or sick and unable to say what treatment they want. Some grown-ups have signed papers that tell whether they want life-support machines used on them if there is no hope that they can get better, or whether they should be allowed to die a natural death without the machines.

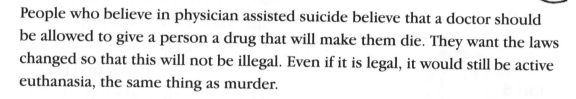

This is how I feel

_____

_____

_____

_____

I Can Help Myself

1. I can write a letter to the editor of a newspaper and say why I believe that euthanasia is wrong.
2. I can ask my parents what I could do to help a family with someone who is dying.
3. I can speak out at school when there is a discussion about physician assisted suicide and explain why it is wrong.

I Can Make Good Choices

1. I can ask my parents what they have decided to do about withholding or withdrawing treatment if they are unconscious and unable to tell the doctor themselves what they want done. And I can ask who the person is who will make the medical decision in the family if one of my parents is not able to do it.
2. During an election I can ask questions about a ballot measures related to euthanasia, so I know what adults will be deciding.
3. I can read the verses in the Bible for myself that describe how God feels about human life, and suffering, and God's promises that He will never give us more than we can stand with His help.

I Can Trust God to Be There for Me

Bible Verse: "I know that a man's life is not his own; it is not for man to direct his steps" (Jeremiah 10:23).

Prayer: Dear God, I want to learn to trust you with everything that happens to me, even hard things, and to remember that you were with me when I was born and will be there when I die. Amen.

The child who has

FAILED

Understanding the Child

Children live in a culture that places too much importance on winning. The idea that winning is the only acceptable outcome is encouraged by adults who are overly invested in the final score in sports competition, or academic grades, or musical performance. They disregard the child's progress, and whether or not the child had a good time. Children mature when they learn from experience that failure may be the motivation for change, and failing at a sport, performance or competition does not mean that the child himself is a failure. Failure is not catastrophic.

Children who experience failure may feel depressed, worthless, guilty for letting others down, embarrassed, hopeless, or inadequate. Girls who fail have more permission to express their feelings and receive support than boys, who may be expected to be strong and not show their feelings.

Children respond in various ways to failure. They may withdraw from their friends, cry, blame others, become bitter, jealous, or excessively angry. Or they may be casual about the failure, focus on their potential to learn, or enjoy the improvement they have shown and whether they had fun. Apart from strong parental influence to take reasonable risks (and therefore risk failure), children may be overly cautious and accept mediocrity and boredom.

Adults who derive excitement and build their own self worth by the successes of their children will inevitably pressure children whether or not they express displeasure at the child's failure.

Children who mature early will often show superior skills in athletic competition, but other children will soon catch up. And the child may then experience some failure.

What YOU Can Do to Help the Child With Failure

1. Discourage blaming, even when others have contributed to the failure. Ask, "What could you do to improve?"
2. Model enjoyment in playing sports or board games even though you lose.
3. Ask, "Did you have fun?" before you ask if the child won.
4. Let the child express his feelings before teaching him the lessons to be learned in failure.
5. Help children improve their skills by offering suggestions about ways to improve and praising the use of these new skills.
6. Compare the child's present performance to the child's past performance to show progress. Don't compare the child's skills to someone who does less well.
7. Tell the child that you respect his effort, that you know how hard he tried, and that you enjoyed watching him practice, even though the outcome was not what the child wanted.
8. Share stories of adults, such as Abraham Lincoln, who had many failures before experiencing success.
9. Point out strengths that the child has. Children who receive poor grades at school may have strong skills in making and keeping friends, etc.
10. Ask the child to think about what is more important than the area of failure, such as their family, being healthy, etc. Winning is not most important.
11. Point out the difference between what God values and the values of the world. God says that being humble and loving others is important. The non-Christian might say that winning is more important.

Conversation Starters

"I noticed that you congratulated the winner. That was really nice. Was it hard for you to do that?"

"How did you feel when you didn't win today?"

"Where do you think you are showing the most improvement in your skills?"

"Some people think that winning is the most important thing, but our family believes that doing your best is what really matters. Did you do your best today?"

Pointing the Child to God

Children need to know that God says anyone who loves and obeys Him is a winner!

EVERYONE FAILS SOMETIMES

Why Does This Hurt So Much?

If you have failed at something that was important to you, you probably feel badly about it. It is hard to lose when you want to win. Everyone fails sometimes. Even the people who look the most successful have had lots of failure.

If you are involved in competition, you are probably spending a great deal of time practicing and thinking about it. Maybe you have not been able to do some of the other fun activities that you would also enjoy because you are busy practicing. You might have mixed-up feelings about that.

How Do Other Kids Feel?

Some kids feel pressured to win because they don't feel good about themselves and winning makes them feel successful. And some kids believe that winning is very important to their parents and they don't want to disappoint them. Sometimes these kids are upset for a whole day after losing, or they have tantrums, or they might even try to cheat to win. No one likes to lose, but winning dishonestly, or calling others bad names, or feeling extremely nervous before competition are clues that winning is overly important.

Some kids are very aggressive in sports and they try to hurt others in order to win. Most kids are afraid of being hurt by these bullies.

This is how I feel

_____

_____

_____

_____

I Can Help Myself

1. I can tell the truth about whether or not I enjoy an activity and I won't participate just because my friends like it.
2. I can remember that no one succeeds without failing at times. The only people who don't fail are those who don't risk learning something new.
3. I can write down all of the things that I do well.
4. After a failure, I can watch a funny movie, play with my friends, hug my dog, or wrap myself in a blanket and read a good book.

I Can Make Good Choices

1. I can decide not to give up just because something is hard. Nobody develops skill without work and practice.
2. When I lose, I will not blame anyone else, have a tantrum, or say bad things about the winner.
3. I can ask a kind adult what would help me improve my skills, so I will be less likely to fail next time.
4. I can ask my parents about a time when they failed, how they felt, and what they learned from the experience.

I Can Trust God to Be There for Me

Bible Verse: "The Lord does not look at the things man looks at. Man looks at the outward appearance, but the Lord looks at the heart" (1 Samuel 16:7).

Prayer: Dear God, help me to remember what is most important. Of course I want to try my best, work hard, obey the rules in everything I do, but most of all I want to please you by my good attitude. Amen.

The child who is

AFRAID

Understanding the Child

Fear is a normal and emotionally healthy response to danger or the threat of danger. Children at certain ages have fears which are common to most children of that age. For example, children who are six months to two years of age are usually afraid of strangers, separation, loud noises, and bright lights. Children three years to seven years are often afraid of going to the doctor, heights, storms, deep water, large animals, insects, or monsters. Children from third grade to early teenage years fear being hurt, school failure, and the possibility of rejection by peers.

Some fears result from warnings by parents, such as how to prevent being kidnapped or to look both ways before crossing streets to prevent being hit by a car.

When a fearful event is anticipated, children can be told what to expect, given direction about what they can do to help themselves, and be offered parental support during the frightening time. Specific fears of childhood often last one year or longer.

Children may deny that they are afraid in an attempt to appear strong and brave in order to please adults.

Some children are by personality more timid and fearful than others. Girls are usually more fearful than boys because they are allowed to express fear without adult disapproval, and because they are given more warnings about things to fear.

Children have the most fears between first and third grades, a time when children normally attach living qualities to inanimate objects (if it moves, it's alive) and their imaginations and fantasy run rampant, as they are most aware of their helplessness to protect themselves from danger.

What YOU Can Do to Help the Child Who Is Afraid

1. Don't make fun of a child's fears by contrasting him to other children his age who are not afraid.
2. Don't reinforce fears by exaggerated protection, such as allowing a child to postpone a dental appointment.
3. Be patient and calm as the child expresses his fear. Don't show annoyance or make fun of the fear.
4. Don't allow a child to manipulate others because he is afraid, such as avoiding outdoor chores for fear of insects.
5. Don't allow young children to watch violent cartoons or scary stories on TV.
6. Give examples of how to handle realistic fears. Say "I am afraid of thunderstorms, so I will stay in the house with the family and keep busy doing something fun until the storm is past."
7. Focus on building the child's confidence to handle fearful events, rather than excessively warning the child about the danger.
8. Don't force a child to have direct contact with a feared object in order to face the fear head on. Allow children to express their fear, give them time to adjust without being rushed, stay with them, tell them what to do to be safe, and reward progress in conquering the fear.
9. Give children many opportunities for accomplishment. Self-confident children have less fear.
10. Talk to the child's pediatrician if strong fears persist.

Conversation Starters

"Would you like me to read you a story about another child who was afraid of the dark and learned how to handle it?"

"What is it about going to the doctor that frightens you?"

"I know that you are afraid you won't get your spelling words right on the test tomorrow. May I help you study?"

"When I was your age, I was afraid of deep water too, so I wore a life vest and took my time getting used to swimming in the deep end of the pool. No one is going to rush you."

"I'm glad that you told me you feel afraid. Let me tell you what is going to happen ..."

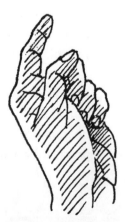

Pointing the Child to God

Children need to know that God cares about everything that matters to them. He has even counted all of the hairs on their heads!

I'M AFRAID!

Why Do I Feel So Afraid?

There are lots of reasons why kids feel afraid. Maybe you haven't been told what will happen in a certain situation, such as going to the hospital for an operation. Anyone would be afraid of the unknown. Or maybe you had a bad experience in the past and you worry that it will happen again. Or maybe you have been warned about something that is dangerous and you were told to be careful, but you don't know exactly what to do to be careful. There are lots of reasons you might feel afraid, but there are also many things that you can do to help yourself feel strong and safe.

Being afraid is nothing to feel ashamed about. It is a challenge to conquer with a little help from your friends.

How Do Other Kids Feel?

Some kids worry more than other kids. Kids who live with adults who have lots of fears are usually more afraid than kids who live with adults who don't have many fears. And kids who watch a lot of scary TV shows are usually fearful. Kids who feel good about themselves have less fear than kids who don't like themselves very much.

Kids like to have adults help them with their fears. It is hard for kids to admit that they feel afraid, but the truth is most kids are afraid of something. Kids like to be told the truth about what will happen, and then to be told what to do to feel less afraid.

This is how I feel

_____

_____

_____

_____

I Can Help Myself

1. I can ask "what if" questions so that I know what to do in a scary situation, such as what I should do if a large dog comes toward me, or what I should do if a bully threatens me.
2. I can ask for an adult to stay close and hold my hand when I'm scared, or tell me a funny story so I forget about being scared.
3. I can ask my parents or teachers what I should be afraid of, and what I don't need to fear.
4. I can learn how to get help if I am alone and afraid, such as by going to a block house or by calling 911.

I Can Make Good Choices

1. I can choose to not allow my fears to control me. I can take little steps in getting more comfortable with what I fear, such as looking at a pet snake without touching it.
2. I won't pretend that I'm not afraid. All kids are afraid at times.
3. I can set standards that are realistic. I won't expect to get an A on every spelling test. I don't have to be afraid of not being perfect.
4. I can lean helpful self-talk, such as, "I know what to do," "I can handle this," or "I'm getting braver."

I Can Trust God to Be There for Me

Bible Verse: "When I am afraid, I will trust in you" (Psalm 56:3).

Prayer: Dear God, thank you for being there in the dark. Amen.

The child who lives in

FOSTER CARE

Understanding the Child

No matter what the circumstances are, living away from their biological parents is hard for children. The reasons for out of home placement may vary, including mental or physical illness of the parent, drug or alcohol abuse, immaturity or lack of parenting skills. Children may be placed by their parents in another home or by the courts as a result of abuse or neglect. Children will grieve the loss of their parents even when they have been rejected, neglected, abused, or abandoned. The child who is asked to choose between an abusive biological parent and a kind, nurturing foster parent, will usually choose the biological parent.

Children feel protective of their biological parents and are hurt by hearing criticism of them, even when they know the criticism is true. Some of the child's identity is linked to his parents.

Children may assume that they will be accepted in the foster home only when they have good behavior. This fear will often result in an initial and temporary "honeymoon" until they feel safe enough to act out their real feelings.

The circumstances of the placement will impact on how the child adjusts to living away from home, as well as how old the child is at the time of placement, whether or not the child is informed prior to placement and gently told the truth about the need for placement; and, whether the child has been told that the biological parents love the child even though they are unable to parent him at the time.

Children who are allowed to visit their biological parents on a regular basis tolerate out of home placement better than those who do not.

What YOU Can Do to Help the Foster Child

1. When the information is known, the child should be told how long you believe the out of home placement will last and what circumstances must occur before the child can safely return home.
2. Tell the child the house rules in the new placement, such as whether or not it is okay for children to get up for a drink of water after going to bed and what are the consequences of disobeying a rule?
3. Tell children that you know they already have parents, but that you will be acting as their parent for awhile to keep them safe and take care of them.
4. Never make any critical remarks about the biological parents in front of the children. Just report facts as it is appropriate, Don't speak for the biological parents. Say, "I love you," not "Your parents love you."
7. Encourage the child to put feelings into words rather than act out the feelings.
8. Allow children to grieve by expressing their anger, hurt, and sadness. Do not expect children to be grateful for the foster placement.
9. Tell children that parents can learn and change, just as children can learn and change.
10. Children with multiple out of home placements may have difficulty forming deep emotional attachments to others. Trust is a skill children learn in preschool years.

Conversation Starters

"Would you like to write your parents a letter and tell them how you are feeling?"

"Why do you believe that you are living in our home right now?"

"What is the hardest thing about living away from your parents?"

"We respect the way your parents are trying to get help for their drug problem."

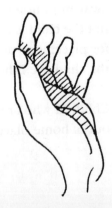

Pointing the Child to God

Children need to know that people who invite Christ into their heart belong to God's forever family.

WHY AM I LIVING IN A FOSTER HOME?

Why Is This So Hard?

You may have a hard time knowing what to say when people ask you why you are living in a foster home. You can say that your parents aren't able to take care of you just now. You don't have to tell them any more information than that.

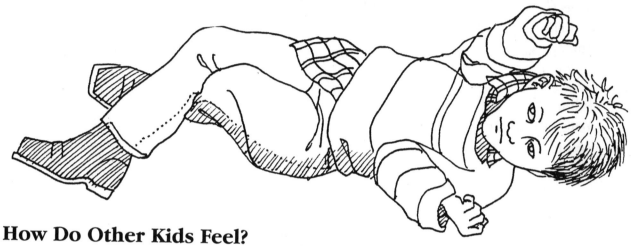

How Do Other Kids Feel?

Sometimes kids wonder if they were placed in foster care because they were bad, but that is not the reason kids live away from home. Kids also worry about whether their parents love them. Biological parents usually love their children very much, even when they are not able to provide day to day care for them.

Kids worry about how their parents are doing and think that they should be there to help them. It is hard for kids to remember that adults take care of adults.

Kids also worry about whether they will be good enough so they won't have to leave the foster home. These are all scary feelings.

This is how I feel ——————

_____

_____

_____

_____

I Can Help Myself

1. I can spend time working on a project that makes me feel good about myself, such as making a present for my biological parents.
2. I can tell the truth about feeling scared and angry and learn what to do with my feelings besides hitting somebody.
3. I can make up happy endings to my nightmares.
4. If my parents don't come for a family visit, I can plan something else that would be fun to do so I won't feel so disappointed.

I Can Make Good Choices

1. I can decide what I want to call my foster parents. It's okay to call them Mom and Dad even though they are just taking care of me for now.
2. I can choose to learn and grow while I am in foster care, just like my parents can learn and grow.
3. I can make a picture album of my time at the foster home. I can ask for a picture of my biological mom and dad for the album too.

I Can Trust God to Be There for Me

Bible Verse: "God is our refuge and strength, an ever-present help in trouble" (Psalm 46:1).

Prayer: Dear God, change is hard for me. Sometimes I feel scared and sad. Thank you for always being there for me. Amen.

The child affected by

GANGS

Understanding the Child

Whatever has happened in the lives of young children or in their families or neighborhoods seems normal to them. Children who live in neighborhoods with gang activity believe that gangs are a part of life.

Children may develop an attitude of gang acceptance in early grade school. They observe the fear and respect given to gang members. They note that money is obtained easily for expensive clothes, and toys. Actual identity with a gang is likely to occur by the time a child is ten years old.

Children who fear gangs may join as a means of self-protection, not because they support the activities of the gang, but because they are afraid not to join. In addition, children from single parent homes with absent fathers may seek gang affiliation simply to provide an authority figure and a clear set of life rules. Children feel safe when "do's and don'ts" are spelled out and when good guys and bad guys are labeled.

Boys may be attracted to gang affiliation because of the extreme emphasis on masculine roles. Boys who live with mothers and sisters may seek a model of tough males.

Children may join gangs because an older sibling has aligned with a particular gang, and the young child feels it is the family tradition. Or a child may join gangs because all of the child's playmates are joining and the child does not want to feel different.

Children who adopt gang mentality may not fully understand that activities of the gang cause suffering for many others and are against the law.

What **YOU** Can Do to Help the Child Affected by Gangs

1. Teach children logical consequences. Carrying weapons, selling drugs, spray painting graffiti, going for joy rides in a stolen car, etc., will all alter the child's opportunities for the future (criminal record) or may result in the child being killed.

2. Tell children clearly why gang activity is wrong. Use Bible verses that tell what God has to say about murder, stealing, lacking respect for authority, etc.

3. Meet the needs of children at risk for gang affiliation:
   a. Provide good adult male models.
   b. Assure the child's physical safety.
   c. Allow children the opportunity to earn money by work.
   d. Give clear structure, rules, boundaries. Be a strong but emotionally available parent.
   e. Help children in developing non gang friendships by inviting these children to your home.
   f. Create a loving and close family; have fun together.
   g. Teach children how to say "no" to peer pressure.
   h. Build a sense of worth, self-respect, and hope.
   i. Communicate your family values.

4. Attend informational meetings sponsored by schools or police departments regarding current gang activity and trends. Tell children what you have learned so they know you are aware and involved in prevention.

5. Honor positive behavior and choices by children.

6. Pay attention to the details of the child's academic, emotional, social, and spiritual life. Don't ignore early signs of difficulty.

7. Talk about gang impact on businesses and about the suffering of families of gang drive-by shootings.

8. Show children how to resolve differences: talk, listen, negotiate, compromise, apologize.

Conversation Starters

"Has anyone ever asked you to join a gang? Would you like some help in how to respond if you are asked?"

"What would you like to be/do when you grow up? Have you thought about what you will need to do to make that happen?"

"Do you know any kids who are in a gang? Why did they join?"

"You make us proud of you. You really make good choices! We are so lucky to have you in the family."

Pointing the Child to God

Children need to know that they belong to the family of God and that they have a strong, kind heavenly Father.

"Your mother and I are going to spend time Saturday painting over graffiti in our neighborhood. Would you like to help?"

A GANG IS A GROUP THAT'S ALWAYS BAD

Why Is This So Hard?

Maybe you live in a neighborhood that has gangs and you are scared about what might happen to you or someone in your family. Or maybe you have just heard about gangs and you know that sometimes innocent people get hurt and that worries you. Gangs are bad and people and property do get hurt. The most important thing is to know how to keep safe and to decide never to join a gang! If you are worried about a gang, you can tell an adult and ask for help. You don't have to try to figure out what to do all by yourself.

How Do Other Kids Feel?

Kids want to learn about gangs. They want to know about gang colors of clothing, and hand signs, and other ways to tell if someone is in a gang. They also want to know why someone would join a gang in the first place. The answer is that there are lots of different reasons why kids join gangs.

Joining a gang is always a choice. Nobody has to do it, even if their older brother is in a gang, or even if someone threatens them and says something bad will happen if they don't join.

One reason kids join gangs is because they want to be a part of a group and have friends who will be on their side. Some groups are good and some groups are bad. Gangs are always bad.

This is how I feel

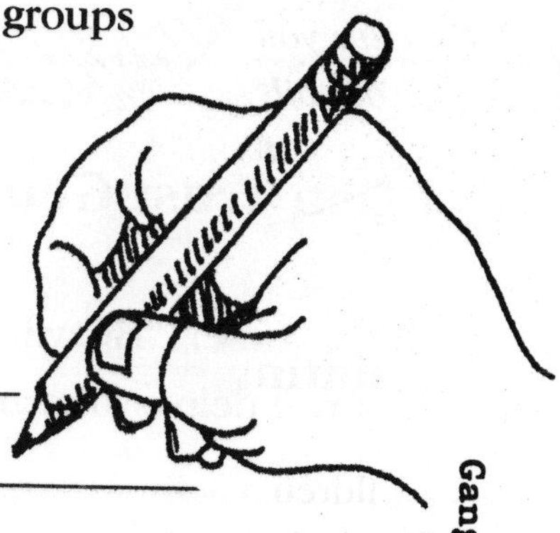

_____

_____

_____

_____

I Can Help Myself

1. I can ask my parents for ideas about how to earn some money by working for it.
2. I can remember that sometimes kids who are in gangs end up in jail, or dead, not rich and powerful like they think.
3. I can learn to do something well, so that I feel good about myself.
4. I can stay away from guns and tell an adult if I see someone with a gun or weapon. I won't keep bad secrets.

I Can Make Good Choices

1. I can stay away from other kids who are involved in a gang and not go to places where gang members might be.
2. I can choose friends who do things I respect. Real friends would never ask me to do something wrong.
3. I can practice saying, "No! I'm not interested" if someone asks me to join a gang or do something wrong.
4. I can avoid stealing, spray painting graffiti, using or selling drugs, wearing gang colors, or looking at violent TV programs or comic books that make violence seem acceptable.

I Can Trust God to Be There for Me

Bible Verse: "He will call upon me, and I will answer him; I will be with him in trouble, I will deliver him and honor him" (Psalm 91:15).

Prayer: Dear God, sometimes I make wrong choices because I am afraid to make the right choice. Please help me to stay away from gangs and keep me safe. Amen.

The child who loves a
HOMOSEXUAL

Understanding the Child

Children are exposed to homosexuality in a variety of
ways. They may live with a single parent who is
openly homosexual; their parents may have
divorced due to the noncustodial parent
coming "out of the closet," they may have an
older sibling who is homosexual, or they
may know a neighbor who is "gay."

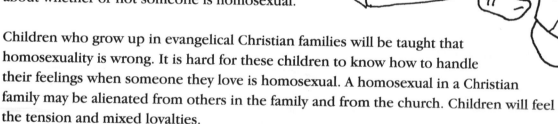

In addition children learn about homosexuality through watching TV, reading about gay
pride parades, listening to their parents discussions about political ballot measures, or
by overhearing whispered conversations
about whether or not someone is homosexual.

Children who grow up in evangelical Christian families will be taught that
homosexuality is wrong. It is hard for these children to know how to handle
their feelings when someone they love is homosexual. A homosexual in a Christian
family may be alienated from others in the family and from the church. Children will feel
the tension and mixed loyalties.

Public school curriculum often includes teaching about homosexuality as a part of
programs which "celebrate diversity." This view will be in contrast to Biblical teaching
which clearly states that homosexual behavior is wrong. Children need guidance and
support in presenting the Christian perspective of loving sinners and hating sin.

Children are curious about sexual issues. They can be told that homosexuality may
have some genetic or hormonal cause, or it may be the result of childhood emotional
trauma, but being born with it doesn't mean that a gay person cannot control his
sexual actions.

What YOU Can Do to Help the Child

1. Children need permission to freely love the homosexual regardless of the adult relationship to the person.
2. Teach children that homosexuality is not worse than other sins and that we are all sinners in need of a Savior.
3. Tell children that Christians need to use good manners and be gracious and kind while presenting their views.
4. Tell children that homosexuality is not contagious.
5. Show children Bible verses that state homosexuality is wrong, but that we are to love, help, and pray for all people, including gays.
6. Review political measures on gay rights issues and tell the child how you will vote and why.
7. Say that all of us have wrong desires at times, but God gives Christians the ability to resist doing wrong things.
8. Teach children that they are never to use unkind slang expressions, such as queer, to refer to homosexuals.
9. Say, "Talking about homosexuality is difficult for me, but I want to answer your questions as well as I can. Please ask abut anything you want to understand."
10. Give children the freedom to accept a wide range of behaviors as normal and not necessarily as homosexual, i.e. some boys like to cook, girls like to compete in sports, etc. Wearing an earring doesn't mean that a man is a homosexual.
11. Tell children that it is normal to be curious about sexual things, but that the sexual behavior of adults is personal. Talk in generalities, not specifics.

Conversation Starters

"Would you like me to bring home some books that present the Christian view of homosexuality?"

"Some people think sexual sin is worse than other sins. What do you think?"

"Have you heard about the Christian organizations that help people leave homosexuality?"

"What did you think about the discussion at school today about gay rights?"

"No, it's not okay to try to arrange a date for a gay friend. Sexual orientation is not something you can change by dating the opposite sex. He needs a support group and professional counseling when he is ready."

Pointing the Child to God

Children need to know that God can help homosexuals to live pure lives, even though their sexual feelings remain.

IS IT OK TO LOVE A PERSON WHO IS HOMOSEXUAL?

Why Does This Hurt So Much?

If you love someone who is a homosexual you might have lots of confusing feelings. Maybe you feel angry, ashamed, and embarrassed if the homosexual is your dad or someone that you love. Usually there have been lots of secrets in families where someone is a homosexual, and family members suspect a problem before they know for sure there is one.

Sometimes there is a divorce in the family because one of the parents admitted they were homosexual. If that happened to you, then you have two big adjustments to face: living with only one parent and knowing one is homosexual.

How Do Other Kids Feel?

Usually kids don't want to talk to other people about a homosexual who they care about. Kids have heard jokes and slang, and unkind remarks about gay people, and now someone they know and love is a homosexual. Kids wonder if it is inherited ("Will I be gay?"), they think it is gross ("How could they do that?"), they feel sad and betrayed ("How could you hurt Mom and us like this?").

Some kids have simple solutions to this very complicated problem. They think a person can just stop homosexual feelings if they really want to. The truth is, even when people want to change, they usually need the help of a professional counselor. They may still have homosexual feelings, but they can stop homosexual behaviors.

This is how I feel

_____

_____

_____

_____

I Can Help Myself

1. I can ask questions instead of worrying and wondering.
2. I can remember that God loves homosexuals and I can too.
3. If someone tries to touch me in a sexual way, whether they are homosexual or heterosexual, I will report it right away.
4. I can find a safe adult to talk to about my feelings and ask for the comfort and help I deserve.

I Can Make Good Choices

1. I can choose to act in loving ways even if I am hurt and confused.
2. When someone tells a mean joke about homosexuals, I can walk away, or remain quiet and not laugh.
3. I can talk to a Christian adult about homosexuality so that when homosexuality is taught at school as an alternative life style, I will know how to respond.
4. I can ask God to help me always obey him in my sexual thoughts and behavior.

I Can Trust God to Be There for Me

Bible Verse: "It is God's will that you should be sanctified; that you should avoid sexual immorality; that each of you should learn to control his own body" (1 Thessalonians 4:3, 4).

Prayer: Dear God, we live in a world that is so full of sin and hurt and wrong. Please come soon and take us to Heaven. In the meantime, help me to honor you with my thoughts and my actions. Amen.

The **HOSPITALIZED** child

Understanding the Child

Children usually are not hospitalized except for serious illness or for surgery, so the event is often abrupt and frightening. Some of the things that frightens adults about hospitalization are: outcome of the illness, cost, impact on employment or self-esteem, but these are rarely issues of concern to children. Children live in the now and their concerns are more immediate ("Will it hurt? Will I have needles?").

Children assume that painful procedures are punishment by adults for the child's wrong doing. Young children cannot understand that something that hurts is for their good. Children are told that doctors help people get better, but the child who feels fine before surgery leaves after a hernia repair feeling much worse, and this too is confusing.

Adults usually prefer the privacy of a single room. Children usually feel better when they are in a room with other children.

Most children have had little experience with basic hospital life: bed pans, food on trays, beds that crank up, side rails, etc. All of these add to the anxiety of being away from home.

One of the most important factors in determining whether the hospital experience will be positive or negative for the child is the attitude of the parent. Parents who do not minimize the real fears of children, and are confident about the quality of medical care and the expected good outcome of the illness or surgery, will communicate their feelings to the child.

What YOU Can Do to Help the Hospitalized Child

1. The younger the child, the more damaging the hospital experience is likely to be. Whenever possible, a loved adult should stay with a young child most of the time in the hospital.
2. Give children simple explanations about what will happen when they go to the hospital. Tell them how long they will be in the hospital, if you expect to stay with them, that the nurse stays awake all night to help children, and you will explain what is happening.
3. Expect that children will regress and so provide comfort by teddy bears, loved blankets, etc.
4. Tell children about a painful procedure just prior to it occurring. Be honest about the fact that it will hurt and compare the hurt to something the child understands, "It will feel like a bee sting."
5. Give children permission to cry and tell them they don't have to be brave and strong all of the time.
6. Take the child for a tour of the hospital pediatric unit prior to the hospitalization if possible. If the hospital has a Child Life Therapist, ask if you can say hello.
7. Don't describe only the interesting, fun experiences which might happen at the hospital: the playroom, a remote control for watching TV in bed, eating Popsicles. Also say that the child's tummy will hurt after the operation, but you will sit nearby to help her.
8. The child who knows someone who has been hospitalized will expect the same outcome with his own hospitalization. If a grandparent died at the hospital, the child may expect that he will also die.
9. There are many children's books about being in the hospital. Reading these books will help children formulate questions, and to know that many other children have wondered the same thing.

Conversation Starters

"Have any of your friends at school been in the hospital before? What did they say about it?"

"Which toys would you like to take to the hospital with you?"

"Do you understand why you need to have this operation?"

"I bought a doctor kit for you. Would you like to pretend you are the doctor and I will be the little boy who has an operation?"

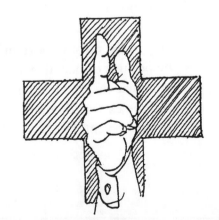

Pointing the Child to God

Children need to know that God uses doctors to help children get better when they are sick.

I'M GOING TO THE HOSPITAL

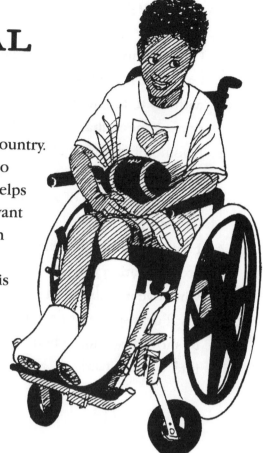

Why Is This So Hard?

Going to a hospital is a little bit like going to a foreign country. So many things are different there! It would be natural to be worried about going to a place that isn't familiar. It helps to remember that people who work in hospitals really want to help kids. Maybe you know someone who has been in the hospital before and you wonder if the same things that happened to them will happen to you? The answer is that some things might be the same, like having your temperature taken, and eating your meals off of a tray and having a bed that goes up and down, but many things will be different.

How Do Other Kids Feel?

When kids know they are going to a hospital for an operation, they usually have mixed feelings. They might feel curious, or scared, or special, or worried.

Most kids know that sometimes the doctor has to do things that hurt and that makes kids worry. Usually doctors or nurses at the hospital will tell you if something is going to hurt, and most of the time the hurt doesn't last very long at all.

When kids have to go to the hospital because they are too sick to stay at home, they don't have time to get used to the idea before they leave. Sick kids already feel bad and they want to know that their mom or dad will stay with them at the hospital.

This is how I feel

_____

_____

_____

_____

I Can Help Myself

1. I will tell myself, "I can handle this."
2. I will give myself permission to sleep with my teddy bear if I want to. It doesn't mean that I am a baby.
3. If something is going to hurt, I will ask someone to tell me a story to keep my mind off of what is happening.
4. I will remember that all of my feelings are okay, and I can tell the people who love me how I am feeling.
5. I will draw pictures or play with clay to show how I feel when I can't put it into words.

I Can Make Good Choices

1. I will tell the nurse when I hurt. She won't know unless I tell her and she can give me medicine to stop the pain.
2. I can learn about my body and how it works by looking at my X-rays or an anatomy book that shows pictures of the inside of the human body.
3. I can save souvenirs from the hospital, like paper medicine cups and my name band, to show at school.
4. If I am in the hospital because of an accident, I can remember that I'm not being punished, and I'm not stupid or unlovable. It was just an accident, and accidents happen.
5. It is okay to ask the same question over and over until I really understand the answer.

I Can Trust God to Be There for Me

Bible Verse: "There is a friend who sticks closer than a brother" (Proverbs 18:24).

Prayer: Dear God, thank you for the doctors and nurses who will help me at the hospital. Help me to remember that you are the Great Physician. Amen.

The child who is

ALONE AFTER SCHOOL

Understanding the Child

The necessary safety precautions set by parents to protect children while they stay alone after school may reinforce the fears that children have about being alone. Caution about not opening the door to strangers reminds children that there are unsafe people who might hurt them.

Children who come home from a "hard day at the office" (school) must delay the opportunity to talk about their day and to be nurtured. When parents do come home from work, they may be exhausted themselves and have limited energy to immediately focus on the happenings of the child's day.

Although there are general guidelines suggested by local state agencies about what age children may safely be left without adult supervision, there are other factors more important than the child's age in determining when the child can be left alone. The child's maturity, the availability of adult resources in the neighborhood, the amount of time the child will be unattended, the child's mental age and history of making appropriate decisions, as well as the child's willingness to be left alone. A child of 14 years may not be mature enough to be left alone, and a ten year old may do just fine.

Approximately 42% of children between the ages of five and nine years of age are left home alone. 77% of older children are left alone. Many come from single parent homes in which the cost of paid after school care is prohibitive. Many children under ten years are consistently left alone, although in most states it is against the law to do so.

In urban communities there are usually before and after school programs available for latch-key children. Survival skills training courses are also available for children who must be alone. Coming home to an empty house may be an economic necessity, but it is always stressful for children and every effort must be made to provide them support.

What YOU Can Do to Help the Latchkey Child

1. Give simple, clear instructions about how to handle various situations, and then role-play "What if . . ."
2. A family dog which is allowed into the house will provide companionship, play, and emotional warmth.
3. The more structured the time alone is for the child, the more secure the child will feel.
4. Young children should not do any cooking while alone. Providing an after school snack and a "love note" from the parent helps.
5. If older siblings are expected to care for younger children, the principle is that the younger the child the older the care-giver sibling must be. A fourteen year old can watch younger children. Children at ten years should not supervise younger children without an adult at home.
6. Leave a list of emergency phone numbers posted by the phone. Write your home address in case the child must tell authorities where you live. Leave names and numbers of relatives or close friends who can care for the children if you have an emergency and can't get home.
7. Leave children alone for increasing amounts of time. Start with one hour, then two hours, etc.
8. Provide written information to nearby adults or relatives, regarding medication the child takes, and doctor's name.
9. Teach children basic first-aid and safety rules. Children may know what to do if a situation is exactly as taught, but not be able to adapt to alterations. If the child is told to never leave the house, they must know that if the stove is on fire, they should run to the neighbor's house.

Conversation Starters

"You will be alone for three hours. Here are the rules to keep you safe. . . . Do you have any questions?"

"How do you feel about being home alone after school?"

"What would you do if someone called and asked if you were home alone?"

"I will phone you from work every day at 4 PM to see how you are doing. I trust you to follow the rules, but I wish I could be at home for you after school instead of talking on the phone."

Pointing the Child to God

Children need to know that when they are worried or afraid,
God is always there.

IT'S SCARY BEING HOME ALONE AFTER SCHOOL

Why Is This So Hard?

You probably feel proud of your parents and the jobs they have. And you probably have friends who are alone after school just like you, but just because staying by yourself is common, it doesn't mean that you necessarily like it. If your parents work, they might have difficulty coming to programs at school. Maybe you wish you could play outside or with your friends after school, but you must stay in the house. One of the ways that kids make friends is spending time with friends playing, so maybe you feel a little lonely.

How Do Other Kids Feel?

Sometimes kids pretend that they are never worried or scared, but most kids wish there was a grown-up around when they get home from school. Sometimes that just isn't possible, even though your parents wish they could be at home when you get there.

Usually when parents leave kids alone it is because they believe that the kids are responsible and will follow the rules. It helps kids to have the rules written down, such as how much time can be spent watching TV cartoons, when homework and chores have to be done, and whether they can talk on the phone. Kids want to know exactly what to do if someone comes to the door, or if they get hurt. Kids feel safer if the rules are clear.

This is how I feel

_____

_____

_____

_____

I Can Help Myself

1. I can ask my parent which adult I should call if I have a problem or question while I am alone.
2. I don't have to protect my parents by denying my feelings about being alone after school. Sometimes nothing can be done to change the situation, but it is okay to talk about my feelings.
3. I can review the safety rules, such as what I should do if I get hurt when I am alone, or if someone asks me to go to the park to play.
4. I can keep a list of emergency phone numbers and the name of the nearest cross streets, and our home address, right by the phone, in case I have to call 911 for a big emergency.

I Can Make Good Choices

1. I won't open the door to an stranger, not even delivery people. And I won't tell anyone on the phone that I am alone. If someone asks to talk to my parent, I'll say that they can't come to the phone now.
2. When I come home from school, I will walk with a friend, and not by myself.
3. I won't use a public bathroom when I am alone, if possible.
4. I will keep busy doing my chores and homework before I watch TV.

I Can Trust God to Be There for Me

Bible Verse: "For God did not give us a spirit of timidity, but a spirit of power, of love and of self-discipline" (2 Timothy 1:7).

Prayer: Dear God, I am so glad that I can always talk to you. I know that I am growing up and I want to please my parents and you with what I do while I am alone. Amen.

The **LONELY** child

Understanding the Child

Children may be lonely for a variety of reasons. They may live in a chronically stressful home and have few opportunities to observe and practice the skills of making and keeping quality friendships. Or they may be temporarily lonely due to a recent move to a new neighborhood. Children may be physically separated from their peers as a result of long-term illness or injury. They may have behavioral problems that interfere with being accepted by others. Children with good self-esteem are not likely to be lonely for long.

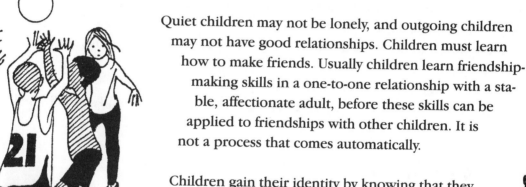

Quiet children may not be lonely, and outgoing children may not have good relationships. Children must learn how to make friends. Usually children learn friendship-making skills in a one-to-one relationship with a stable, affectionate adult, before these skills can be applied to friendships with other children. It is not a process that comes automatically.

Children gain their identity by knowing that they belong in a family, Sunday school classroom, neighborhood, school, or with peers. It is more important that children have several good friends than to have many superficial acquaintances.

Helping children develop friendships and combating loneliness must begin by observing what difficulties the child has with other children and then responding specifically. The skills needed for the child who has just moved to a new neighborhood are quite different than those needed by the child who has not learned to share and is therefore rejected by others. Children who are separated from loved friends in another town can learn creative ways to sustain the relationships through letters, phone calls, pictures, and audio tapes.

What YOU Can Do to Help the Child

1. Point out the probable feelings of others so that children can learn empathy.
2. Teach children how to resolve differences. Sharing, apologizing, taking turns, or walking away if the child feels especially angry are needed skills which can be learned.
3. Tell the child what you especially enjoy when you are with them. Say, "I like the way you shared your truck."
4. Introduce the child to all guests in the home. It teaches children how to meet strangers and communicates to them that you recognize their importance.
5. Enroll the child in group activities, such as swimming, gymnastics, soccer or provide lessons in music or art.
6. Read stories about other shy or lonely children who found solutions to their loneliness and suggest that the child try one of the helpful ideas in the book.
7. Help children learn to discuss a variety of topics. Talking with an attentive adult gives children practice in what to talk about with peers.
8. Teach children how to tell age-appropriate jokes.
9. Give verbal praise for efforts to sustain conversation, such as asking others questions, giving compliments, paying attention.
10. Suggest finding another shy child and asking about a particular TV show, as a beginning to conversation.
11. Invite families with same age children to come over for dinner.
12. Teach children to be considerate, remember others' names, smile and say hello first, show interest in what others are doing.

Conversation Starters

"Sharing is hard for you. That may be why you feel lonely. What could you do to remember to let others have a turn?"

"What are some of the fun things you would like to do with a friend?"

"Let's practice how to get acquainted with someone you would like to know."

"Would you like to invite someone to go with our family to the beach on Saturday?"

"If you would like to take gymnastics, your dad and I will pay for the lessons. What do you think?"

Pointing the Child to God

Children need to know that Jesus had some special friends and knows that kids need special friends too. He understands loneliness.

SOMETIMES I FEEL LONELY

Why Is This So Hard?

Everybody needs friends, so if you are feeling lonely this must be a hard time for you. Maybe you feel that you are different from the other children in your school, or maybe you feel very shy inside and it is hard to talk to kids you don't know yet. Maybe you just don't know how to make friends. Even good friends sometimes hurt others feelings by saying something unkind, so it is important to learn how to ask for forgiveness and to make up after a disagreement. People who don't learn how to do this, will always be lonely.

If you are lonely, you need to know that lots of other kids have felt just like you, and that you are not alone. You deserve to have good friends, and you can learn how to be a good friend to someone else. Is there someone else in your Sunday school class or at school who is lonely and needs a friend like you?

How Do Other Kids Feel?

Nobody wants to play alone all of the time. Everybody wants friends to talk to, and play with, and go with to parties. Kids need someone to talk to about homework at school. Usually when kids are lonely, they feel badly about themselves. Sometimes kids don't know why they don't have friends, and sometimes they do know, such as when they have just moved to a new school and left all of their good friends behind. Lonely kids feel sad. Kids can learn how to make friends if an adult helps them.

This is how I feel

_____

_____

_____

_____

I Can Help Myself

1. I can ask someone who loves me what qualities I have that another child would like?
2. I can remember that I am worth knowing, and that I have a lot to offer others.
3. I can take the initiative in making friends and not wait for others to come to me.
4. I can make friends with an adult and learn the skills I need for making friends, such as how to say that I am sorry when I have said something hurtful.

I Can Make Good Choices

1. I can watch other children who have lots of friends and notice what they do to make and keep friends.
2. I can volunteer to work on a project at church or school where there will be other kids. It is easier to work with someone that I don't know well, than to just talk to them.
3. I can learn some topics to talk about, such as "What TV show did you watch last night?"
4. I can say kind things to others, help them, and be friendly. I can invite someone to do something with me.

I Can Trust God to Be There for Me

Bible Verse: "There is a friend who sticks closer than a brother" (Proverbs 18:24).

Prayer: Dear God, thank you for being my best friend, and for always listening to me, and going with me wherever I go. I need a people friend too, God. Please help me learn how to be a friend to others. Amen.

The child who lives with a
MENTALLY ILL ADULT

Understanding the Child

The impact of mental illness on the child will vary based on the type of mental disorder, as well as the age of the child at the onset of the illness, and the quality and amount of support available to the child from other adults.

Many serious mental disorders involve remissions and exacerbations. The adult is functional and able to parent at times, alternating with episodes of serious behavioral problems and limited ability to perform parenting tasks.

Many mental illnesses have a slow onset of symptoms and it is not always clear in the beginning that the parent is mentally ill.

Some mental illnesses include being out of touch with reality, and some are characterized by excessive anxiety. Some involve physical illness which has resulted from emotional problems, and others involve extreme changes in mood, such as being aggressive and angry or depressed. The child who lives with a chronic schizophrenic parent will have very different issues than the child who lives with a parent with Post Traumatic Stress Disorder.

Children need to know that a mental illness is a disease like any other disease. Some mental illnesses are inherited, some result from overuse of alcohol or drugs, some occur because of painful events that occur early in life, and some are caused by accidents or infections of the brain. Children with healthy parenting early in life, cope better than children who have a mentally ill parent at the time of birth.

What YOU Can Do to Help the Child Living With a Mentally Ill Adult

1. Children are frightened when they realize that an adult is not able to be in charge. Then children need rules and boundaries set by other adults.

2. Children may be accused of behavior they have not done or become the recipients of blame for the parents problems, i.e. "You drive me crazy." Children need clear affirmation that this is not true, and that the parent's behavior is caused by the illness.

3. Children may need to live intermittently with other adults (such as grandparents) during hospitalizations of the sick parent. This change is also stressful and involves learning new household rules. Review the rules frequently.

4. Children are embarrassed by the behavior of a mentally ill parent, and peers may tease the child about the parent's actions. Children need comfort and reassurance. Other children need information about mental illness.

5. When the parent is hospitalized, children may experience fear when they visit the parent, both because of the unusual behavior of the parent but also because of the other sick adults at the hospital. Children should be invited to talk about how they feel after hospital visits.

6. Children who are very frightened initially, may act out in anger when the parent's illness is under control. Fear in children often hides anger. Fear that is expressed will decrease anger.

7. Parents who have serious mental illness frequently withdraw from the tasks of daily living into their own private thoughts. Other adults must provide parenting, both at church and at school.

8. Children need to be told what is being done to help the parent, including how medications work, simple explanations of electro-convulsive treatments, counseling, art and drama therapy, and learning ways to reduce stress. The more the child understands, the more the mystery of the illness is removed.

Conversation Starters

"Sometimes kids think that they are responsible for their parent's illness, or that they have to do something to make their parent well, but that isn't true."

"Do you have questions about your daddy's mental illness? I would like to help you find the answer. If I don't know, I will ask someone who does. You deserve to know."

"I know that you visited your mom at the psychiatric hospital today. Would you like to tell me about it?"

"Have you talked about using non prescription drugs or alcohol at school and how it impacts on a person's mental health?"

Pointing the Child to God

Children need to know that one of the ways God shows His love for us is in providing people to help us when we cannot help ourselves.

MY PARENT IS MENTALLY ILL

Why Is This So Hard?

If you are living in a family with a mentally ill adult, you may have had some difficult experiences that other children have never had. Even though you might not know other children with a mentally ill adult, there are thousands and thousands of children who live with a mentally ill adult and have the same kinds of questions and concerns that you have.

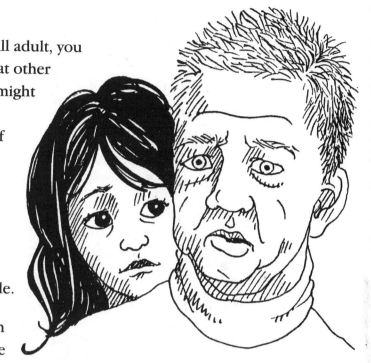

A mentally ill adult may not be able to take care of all of your needs and you probably need help from other caring adults for awhile.

Being hurt or mad at the mentally ill adult in your family doesn't mean that you don't love them. You can be mad at someone and love them at the same time.

How Do Other Kids Feel?

When parents are mentally ill, they may not be able to give children directions. At first kids might think it is great that their parent isn't telling them what to do, but soon they find out that it is scary when an adult is not in charge. Kids need someone to set the rules, to keep them safe, to require eating only healthy food, and to make them go to bed in time to get plenty of sleep.

Kids learn that having a mentally ill parent is hard, but it is not the very worst thing in the whole world. Kids can learn how to handle this tough situation.

This is how I feel

_____

_____

_____

_____

I Can Help Myself

1. I can learn to call 911 if there is an emergency at my house with the mentally ill adult.
2. I can make a list of five adults that I can go to for help.
3. I can learn the difference between safe and unsafe behaviors in the mentally ill parent.
4. I can read Bible verses about how much God loves everyone, including the mentally ill adult in my family.
5. I can read a children's book about mental illness.

I Can Make Good Choices

1. I can remember that it is not my responsibility to take care of an adult.
2. I can learn what to do when I have sad, lonely, angry feelings myself.
3. I don't have to apologize for the mentally ill adult's behavior. I can control my own behavior but not that of another person.
4. I can develop close, loving relationships with friends.

I Can Trust God to Be There for Me

Bible Verse: "We who are strong ought to bear with the failings of the weak" (Romans 15:1).

Prayer: Dear God, help me to do things that are healthy for my body and my mind, and to trust you with the things that I cannot control in myself and others. Amen.

The child learning about

MENTAL RETARDATION

Understanding the Child

Children may live with a mentally retarded adult, they may know someone who is mentally retarded, or they may be retarded themselves. One out of every ten families in the United States has a mentally retarded person in the family.

Retardation results from a variety of causes, including birth trauma, Down syndrome, or other brain diseases. Some children will have extreme developmental delays that are caused by emotional deprivation or abuse. The delayed child functions like a retarded child, but with time, nurture and stimulation, many of these children can gradually become normal in their intellectual ability.

Retarded children can learn to function at the highest possible level of their neurological potential. Whatever the behavior and level of functioning, the retarded child is probably capable of growing and becoming more skilled.

Maintaining a balance of accepting the child for who he is and not pressuring him to make impossible changes, while at the same time stimulating him mind to stretch to his potential, is the challenge of helping the retarded child.

Retardation ranges from mild to profound. Mildly retarded children will likely be able to complete sixth grade at school.

Parents may not know that the child is retarded until the child is unable to learn what other children at the same age are learning. Since much praise is given to early developmental skills in children, parents of the retarded child may feel discouraged.

What YOU Can Do to Help the Retarded Child

1. Show respect for the child. It will provide an appropriate model for other children, validate the child's worth, and encourage the parents.

2. Respond to the child at the child's developmental level, not chronological age. The ten-year-old child who acts like a two year old, should be treated like a two year old.

3. Allow parents to grieve the loss of potential of their child while recognizing that feeling sad does not mean they love the child less than a one who is not retarded.

4. Allow the retarded child to teach other children to see the world from her perspective. Listen, affirm the child's opinion, and do not tolerate any teasing by others.

5. Recognize that retarded children may be at their developmental age in some skills and below age in other skills. Don't stereotype.

6. Retarded children are not necessarily more loving, tolerant, brave, or happier than any other children.

7. Do not tolerate misbehavior from the retarded child that is not allowed by other children. Rules usually must be kept simple and reinforced again and again.

8. Include retarded children in musical and stage productions.

9. Retarded children often enjoy action more than sitting passively. Adapt classroom teaching to include acting out stories, showing visual aids, and talking in literal descriptions, rather than abstract (hidden) meanings. Say exactly what you mean.

Conversation Starters

"Retarded children are not more special than other children. Every child is special to God. Let's name some ways that you are special."

"I liked the way you included Joey in your play at recess. Did you enjoy being helpful?"

"Sometimes I am very busy taking care of your retarded brother. Would you like some private time with just the two of us?"

"I love to watch you do your very best, and I love to watch your sister do her very best."

"Sometimes kids use slang expressions that make mentally retarded people feel badly about themselves. What could you say or do if you hear someone say something unkind to a retarded person?"

Pointing the Child to God

Children need to know that God looks on our hearts and not our beauty or brains. Retarded children can love God as much as any other child.

TELL ME ABOUT MENTAL RETARDATION

Why Is This So Hard?

You can't always tell by looking at someone whether or not they are retarded. To be retarded simply means that a person has lower than average intelligence. They have less ability to learn some things than a person who is not retarded.

If you know someone who is retarded, then you probably already know that retarded people have all of the same feelings as everybody else. They are more like you than different from you. Retarded kids are sometimes jealous, mad, silly, or scared just like everyone else.

If you live with a retarded person, you know that they need more help than others in the family. It is easy to resent the time that your parents have to take to provide that care. It helps to remember that the retarded person would rather be normal any day, and that your help is very much appreciated. God sees you when you are helping.

How Do Other Kids Feel?

Lots of families have a family member that is retarded. It is very common. Most kids feel protective of the retarded person. If someone makes fun of the retarded person, it hurts everyone in the family.

Sometimes kids have to help out more at home because their mother is very busy helping the retarded child. When that happens, kids might wish they could go out and play like their friends.

Kids might feel guilty about the retardation and wonder if there was anything they did that caused the retardation. Kids can't make someone else retarded.

This is how I feel

_____

_____

_____

_____

I Can Help Myself

1. I can help my retarded family member by:
   a. Giving directions one step at a time.
   b. Showing her how to do something, not telling her.
   c. Praising him when he does something well.
   d. Saying the same thing over and over until it is learned.
2. Being patient when it would be easier to give up.
3. I can explain to my friends about the retardation and how to be helpful.
4. I can play with my friends without feeling guilty.

I Can Make Good Choices

1. I can attend the special athletic tournaments for retarded people to show my support.
2. I can learn about retardation by reading stories about it and by asking the special education teacher at my school to tell me about it.
3. I can remember that everybody needs help with some tasks.

I Can Trust God to Be There for Me

Bible Verse: "Accept one another, then, just as Christ accepted you" (Romans 15: 7).

Prayer: Dear God, sometimes I worry about what will happen to the retarded person in my family. Help me to live one day at a time. Amen.

The child learn to manage
MONEY

Understanding the Child

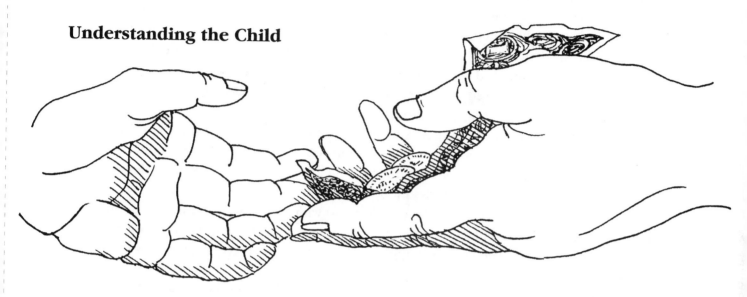

80% of American adults say they don't understand money management, banking, or investments. It is difficult for parents to communicate clear information and direction to children when they have difficulty with money themselves. The need for money places great stress on the family. Differences about how money should be spent is the number one reason for parental divorce. Many parents do not live on a budget or maintain regular savings each month, so asking children to do this is difficult.

Shopping or spending time at the mall is the favorite hang out for most teen-age girls. Children grow up in a highly materialistic culture and by the time children enter first grade they attach value to wealth. Even in Christian families, children grow up believing that money is theirs to spend without understanding that all that we have belongs to God and is ours only to manage.

Young children are confused by credit cards. Purchases can be made without having any money, and the same card buys a shirt or a dinner at the restaurant. Simply by signing your name, you can have anything you want. The reality of paying the bill later and of paying additional money for using the card (interest) is not comprehended.

The decision about when and how much allowance to give children, and what they are required to do with the money, should be decided by the time children enter first grade. It is helpful for children to share the work of the family simply because they belong. Children should not grow up expecting to be paid for every job they do. They can earn money by doing extra jobs beyond basic chores.

Money is a part of life. Children must learn to mange it or it will manage them.

What **YOU** Can Do to Help the Child Manage Money

1. Teach children that they are responsible to maintain what they purchase, i.e. a child who buys a shirt that must be hand washed, should wash it himself.

2. Keep humble. Tell children about the most worthless and unnecessary purchase you have made. Don't imply that you have always made good decisions.

3. Allow children to control how they use spending money. The only way that children can learn to manage money is by experiencing the consequences of their choices.

4. Give children an allowance beginning in the first grade. Tell children it must be divided equally between savings, tithe, and spending. Some parents give one-half the dollars per age of the child each week. A six year old would receive $3.00 a week, and therefore save $1.00, give $1.00, and spend $1.00 anyway the child chooses.

5. The child's spending money should be kept in the child's room and accessible to the child. Use jars, envelopes, or small boxes for money. Savings can be taken to the bank once a month.

6. If children do not manage the money as directed, the parent should review the rules and avoid rescuing the child by giving extra money.

7. Write a written contract about what the child is to do with the allowance. Children should be able to borrow from a parent, as long as interest is charged and the money is re-paid before more can be borrowed. The same rule applies for parents who borrow from children!

8. Help children figure out how to earn extra money.

9. Older children can be given an additional allowance to pay for clothing and school lunches. If the child spends all of the money on a purse and needs a sweater, parents can take the child to a thrift store or loan her the money and charge interest.

Conversation Starters

"I know that you really want to buy it and that you have already spent your money. You won't be able to borrow from me because you are still paying back your debt. Would you like some help in managing your money better?"

"Have you asked God about how to spend the money?"

"Which charity would you like to help support with your "giving" money?

"If you save your spending money for one more week, you can buy it. I like the way you decide what is important to you and then wait for it. You could teach some grown ups!"

Pointing the Child to God

Children need to know that anything, including money, that takes the place of God in our lives is wrong.

HOW TO BE HAPPY ABOUT MONEY

Why Is This So Hard?

Money is important to everyone. Usually the amount of money you have is kept private within a family. You probably have gotten some of your ideas about money from watching your parents. If they enjoy using their money to help others and to support the church, you have learned a good lesson. It is hard to save money, easy to borrow money, and tempting to spend all of the money on yourself. If you receive an allowance, you are making some decisions about what is really important to you by the way you spend the money.

How Do Other Kids Feel?

When kids are little they sometimes think that their parents are rich and can buy anything they want. It takes awhile for kids to understand that grown-ups have to pay lots of bills. Another confusing thing about money is the use of credit cards. Some kids think that using a credit card is the same as using cash, but of course it isn't. It takes a while to learn that it costs far more to use a credit card because of paying the interest added to the bill.

Some kids think that having lots of money would make them happy. The truth is, money doesn't always make people happy, and learning to give money feels very good!

This is how I feel

_____

_____

_____

_____

I Can Help Myself

1. I realize that I won't be paid for getting good grades but I want to do the best I can because it is the right thing to do, not because I will get money for it.
2. When I spend all of my money and then need some more, I can think about what to do to prevent the problem from happening again.
3. I can recognize that it is not my job to worry about my parents finances. It is my job to learn to manage my own money well.
4. I can learn about money by looking at the restaurant bill and figuring out how much tip should be left, by going with my parent to the bank to make deposits, and by comparing prices at a store for similar products.

I Can Make Good Choices

1. I can use my "giving away money" to buy a pair of socks for a homeless person or a New Testament for a child in another country, or I can put it in the offering at church.
2. I can help with the chores at home because I belong to the family and need to do my part to help. I won't expect to get paid for raking the leaves anymore than my mom gets paid for cooking dinner.
3. I can learn about spending money on things that are made well and won't break down the first day. Cheaper is not always better.
4. I can ask for suggestions about how to earn additional spending money, such as washing our neighbor's car or playing with their young children while they are busy.

I Can Trust God to Be There for Me

Bible Verse: "For the love of money is a root of all kinds of evil. Some people, eager for money, have wandered from the faith and pierced themselves with many griefs" (1 Timothy 6:10).

Prayer: Dear God, I want to manage money in a way that makes you happy. Please help me to save, to give, and to spend my money in ways that please you. Amen.

The child who is
MOVING

Understanding the Child

Moving to a new city is stressful for children, but it does not have to be a traumatic event. Children feel most secure in their familiar routine which is interrupted by moving. Even when there are positive features to the move, such as acquiring a room alone, or living near cousins, or being close to the mountains and snow; children will experience some grief at the loss of special friends, their status on the soccer team, the security of being liked by their Sunday school teacher, and knowing what will happen next. Children will also feel the anxiety, exhaustion, and disruption of the lives of their parents who are packing and preparing for the move.

Approximately ten million children in the United States move each year. Even when children experience repeated moves, there does not seem to be any long-range emotional trauma to children if their needs are met before, during, and after the move. Children can have many positive growth producing experiences as a result of moving which they might not have otherwise, such as learning that they can adjust and make friends wherever they live.

Children who have had at least one prior move generally adjust better to moving than children who have lived all of their lives in one location.

The most important factor in helping children adjust to moving is communication with their parents throughout the moving process including information about the physical aspects of the move, permission to verbally grieve their losses, and some thoughtful planning to assist in the adjustment in the new setting.

What YOU Can Do to Help the Child Who Is Moving

1. Tell children that you feel a little bit scared too, but don't discuss major fears, such as financial worries related to the move. Talk about those fears with adults.
2. The concerns of children will focus on themselves. If children have not seen the new house, take a picture or a video tape of their room, play room, backyard.
3. Allow children to make some decisions, such as choosing the color of paint for their new room.
4. Buy an address book for the child and list addresses, phone numbers and, if possible, a small photo of each of the important friends in the former community.
5. Tell children they can call one friend each week from their former town. State the day and time for the call.
6. If possible, schedule a return trip to the former town so children know they will see friends again, even if this visit is a year away. Or schedule a visit from a best friend to come for a two week visit to your new home next summer.
7. Let your child decide what is important to keep and what possessions can be thrown away as you pack.
8. Plan a good-bye party before leaving town and invite the child's friends. Give each guest a T-shirt from the new town where the child will live, along with the child's new address.
9. If possible, schedule the move during the semester break of the school year, not during the summer. Children have an easier time making friends and getting involved in activities.
10. Ask the chamber of commerce in the new city to send information about activities of interest to the child, such as ballet or swim classes. If possible, enroll the child prior to the move.

Conversation Starters

"Would you like to use my camera and take pictures of your new neighborhood to send to your friends where we used to live?"

"Would you like to go to the new school and see the playground?"

"As soon as we are unpacked, let's have a party and invite some kids over. Who would you like to invite?"

"Tell me how you liked your new Sunday school class. Your opinion matters to us."

"Tell me how you feel about moving."

Pointing the Child to God

Children need to know that the family of God lives in every city.

WHY DO WE HAVE TO MOVE?

Why Is This So Hard?

Moving to a new city is filled with lots of unknowns. You might feel excited and think that moving is fun. And you might also feel really sad about leaving your good friends. Maybe you are a little worried about whether you will find friends in the new town, and what the new school will be like. You will definitely have lots of changes! Adults usually have some of the same feelings that you have.

It usually takes awhile to get used to a new house and neighborhood, so please try to be patient with yourself while you get used to everything. You just might find some happy surprises in the new town!

How Do Other Kids Feel?

Kids usually want to learn everything they can about the place they will live, such as: Is there a place I can ride my bike? Will I be able to play softball? Are there kids my age in our new neighborhood? Can I take all of my toys? What does my new room look like? And it helps kids to have answers to these questions because they feel more in control.

Usually on moving day when the house is completely empty, and kids walk through it one last time, they feel sad. It feels like the end of a chapter in a book, and they don't know what the next chapter will be about.

This is how I feel

_____

_____

_____

_____

I Can Help Myself

1. I will pack a small bag of my favorite toys to keep with me for the move. It will give me something to play with until my toys are unpacked.
2. I will pretend this is a treasure hunt and look for all of the good things about the new house and neighborhood.
3. I will read some stories from the library about other children who have moved, so I can learn how they felt.
4. I will take time to say good-bye to my friends and promise them that I will write a letter soon.

I Can Make Good Choices

1. I can decide what I want to keep and what I want to throw out. Then I can put my name on the boxes filled with my things or draw a picture of me on each box.
2. I can make a time capsule with my friends before I move. We can put in written messages about being friends, some pictures of us together, and a story about the things we did together. Then we'll bury it in the backyard.
3. I can ask if our family can keep the same routines that we had before the move, such as going to a movie on Sunday afternoon every week.
4. I can ask if I can be the first one to go into the new house when we arrive.

I Can Trust God to Be There for Me

Bible Verse: "If I settle on the far side of the sea, even there your hand will guide me, your right hand will hold me fast" (Psalm 139:9, 10).

Prayer: Dear God, I am so glad that there is no place I can go that you are not there first. Please protect all of our things in the moving van and us. Help me to find a friend, and be a friend. Amen.

The child dealing with
MURDER

Understanding the Child

Children who know someone who was murdered often experience secondary trauma when they observe the repeated television and newspaper coverage of the event. The more tragic the event, the more likely that gory details will be shown. The death alone is horrible, but viewing the graphic details accentuates the pain. In addition, some statements may be slanderous and inflammatory to the victim.

Sudden, unexpected deaths are experienced differently than death that is anticipated. Initially, adults may respond with numbness and appear more "together" than they will be in the weeks and months that follow.

How the family is informed of the murder will impact how the child and others respond. Usually accurate information is gradually discovered and not all available initially. Parents who are given information gently and with accuracy will be more able to care for the emotional needs of their children.

A murder, or any other tragedy, rarely draws a family together. It is a highly stressful event and children are sometimes neglected while adults try to emotionally survive.

Parents who are preoccupied with the murder, may spend less time with their children in explaining what is happening. In addition, parents may become overly protective of their children and increase the child's fear about living in an unsafe world.

Parents who become bitter and angry following a murder create a home climate that lacks security and warmth for children.

What YOU Can Do to Help the Child

1. Assist children with school work since the ability to concentrate is damaged by fear and grief.
2. Monitor and discuss television and newspaper coverage. Don't try to protect children from the public information. Invite their questions.
3. Avoid using children to meet emotional needs of adults by overly talking about rage, the injustice of the event, and possible desire to retaliate.
4. Give children factual information about grief so they can combat the well-meaning but harmful advice to put it all behind them and get on with life.
5. Explain the judicial system, specifically the role of the defense attorney for the person who is accused of the murder, and who may attempt to slander the victim.
6. Tell children that normal feelings following a murder include: shock, helplessness, terror, rage, guilt, depression; and physical symptoms, such as exhaustion, difficulty sleeping and concentrating, loss of appetite, dry mouth, and accident proneness.
7. Children are confused to find that the good guys don't always catch the bad guys and put them in jail. Children must grieve their loss of faith in the justice system.
8. Tension between parents following a murder will add to the fear and stress for the child. The divorce rate is high. Children need other stable, calm, affectionate adults for support.
9. Children may experience some loss of faith in God to protect them and the people they love. Children need to hear that God cares, and that because we live in a sinful world, some people make bad choices.

Conversation Starters

"Some kids feel guilty going out to play when the whole family is so sad. Have you ever felt that way?"

"What do you wish you knew about the murder?"

"What are the best ways for grown-ups to help kids after something terrible happens?"

"What are some of the feelings kids have after someone they love is murdered?"

"Would you like me to tell you about what will happen in the courtroom?"

Pointing the Child to God

Children need to know that God wants people to be real about how they feel. He understands all the feelings we have.

SOMEONE I KNOW WAS MURDERED

Why Does This Hurt So Much?

If someone that you know has been murdered, you are probably feeling scared, angry, worried, and sad. Anyone would feel that way after someone they loved was murdered. Maybe you feel unsafe walking home from school or playing outside like you used to do. And maybe you have had some nightmares since the murder. It is okay to need some extra help right now.

It takes a long time for a family to recover after someone they love has been murdered, but everyone can learn to be happy again.

You might have lots of questions about the murder. It is okay to ask about anything that is unclear. You have a right to know. Some questions will be hard to answer, such as why did something so terrible happen in my family. These questions don't have human answers. We know that God will be with us in whatever happens in our lives.

How Do Other Kids Feel?

Most kids have watched lots of stories on TV in which someone was murdered, but they have no idea how awful it is when it really happens in their own family. Most kids have never even thought much about the families of the victims after a murder.

Most kids think that everything will be back to normal after the murderer is caught and goes to prison, but usually that isn't true. The people in the family continue to hurt.

This is how I feel

_____

_____

_____

_____

I Can Help Myself

1. I can tell people the truth about how I feel when they ask.
2. I can ask an adult to explain words I don't understand, such as plea bargain, jury trial, defense attorney.
3. I can pray for my family, the attorney, the people on the jury, and myself.
4. I can remember that there is nothing I could have done to prevent the murder. I may feel guilty, but I am not.

I Can Make Good Choices

1. I can go outside to play if the grown-ups are very angry and I feel upset by it.
2. I can ask my parents if there is a support group for children who are feeling sad about a murder of someone they love.
3. I can take my anger out in safe places, such as hitting my pillow or kicking a soccer ball.
4. I can go to the funeral, and I can cry.

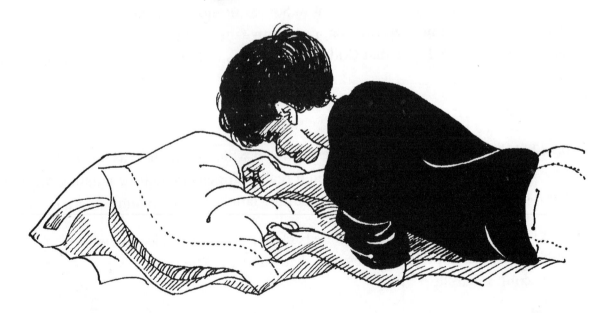

I Can Trust God to Be There for Me

Bible Verse: "You shall not murder" (Exodus 20:13).

Prayer: Dear God, I don't understand why something so sad happened in our family. Help me to learn to trust you with all that I don't understand. Amen.

The child who has experienced a
NATURAL DISASTER

Understanding the Child

Natural disasters can be terrifying because children often experience multiple losses and because they do not have time to emotionally prepare for the event. Children find security in their adult care givers, but during a natural disaster care givers may be frightened, angry, hysterical or emotionally unavailable to comfort the child in their preoccupation with the unfolding events.

Children recognize the random impact of fire, floods, earthquakes, and know that there is little they can do to protect themselves. Their neighbor's house may be unharmed while their own house is burned to the ground.

Families are often separated during the disaster or following it, and children are sent to a safer place. This separation, although necessary, creates additional stress.

It is difficult for children to find relief from the constant barrage of TV, radio, and newspaper accounts of the disaster, along with the persistent discussion about the event by the adult members of their family.

Adults may place all of the focus of attention on the physical safety of children and neglect the psychological aid they need following a disaster.

During the event, children may be more quiet, clingy, obviously frightened, bewildered, or in shock. Following this initial reaction, children may have sleep difficulties and fear separation from their parents to go to school. They may express their feelings about the disaster in their play, be especially fearful of other change, and regress to earlier levels of behavior. These are all common expected responses.

What YOU Can Do to Help the Child

1. Expect that two siblings in the same family will have very different responses to a disaster.
2. Seek professional support for children who have extreme stresses when parents die in a disaster. There may be other family problems such as alcoholism or abuse which prevent care givers form being a source of comfort for children.
3. Involve children in cleaning up following the disaster. It will combat a sense of helplessness.
4. Keep the family physically together if at all possible.
5. Summarize news information in a simple way. Say what will happen next, if you know. State what the family plans to do, i.e. "If the water comes to the ridge, we will drive to Grandma's house." Say when you expect life to return to normal.
6. Let children take comfort items to temporary shelters, such as teddy bears, blankets, etc.
7. Encourage children to put feelings into words regarding losses of friends or pets. Don't overly value being brave.
8. Establish a set routine for the child as soon as possible. Regular meals and bedtime allow children some security.
9. Admit that the event is a terrible thing. Don't minimize the seriousness of the disaster, but assure children that you are able to take care of them.
10. Don't leave children with a neighbor while you go to inspect the damage. Take children with you. Include children in the family sorrow.
11. Comfort children by physically holding them and spending focused time with them.

Conversation Starters

"After the flood is over, we will rebuild another house. How would you like to decorate your new room?"

"Of all the things you lost in the fire, what is the hardest for you?"

"I am crying because I feel so sad about losing our wedding pictures. What makes you sad?"

"Your mom and I will tell you whenever we hear anything new. In the meantime, please ask anything about anything that concerns you."

"What questions do you have?"

Pointing the Child to God

Children need to know that God stays awake all night and they can go to sleep.

DISASTERS ARE SCARY

Why Is This So Hard?

A disaster is very scary! Some of the reasons you might be upset are different from your parents. You might be the most worried about what has happened to your cat, and your parents might be most worried about whether the insurance will pay for the damage.

Usually grown-ups are busy following a disaster and they have less time than usual to explain what is happening.

When everything is all over, you might have a hard time going back to school because you don't want to be separated from your family. It is okay to talk about those feelings.

How Do Other Kids Feel?

Most kids have a hard time knowing the difference between real danger and possible danger during or following a disaster. They don't always know what to worry about.

Kids like to talk to their friends when something scary is happening, but during a disaster they usually can't use the phone or see their friends. Sometimes their friends have been hurt and they are worried and sad about that.

Kids remember different parts of the disaster at different times after it is all over. Lots of kids think and talk about what happened for years afterwards.

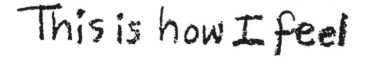

_____

_____

_____

_____

I Can Help Myself

1. I can stay with a comforting grown-up and ask questions about things that worry me.
2. I can go to another room and play when I have heard enough of the news reports on TV. I can take time outs from the disaster when I need to.
3. I can make a notebook about the disaster, draw pictures of what happened, write a report about it, pretend I am a reporter and interview people about the disaster, and cut out newspaper articles.
4. I can be patient with myself. This is a very hard experience and I need time to accept it. Talking about it will help me. Remembering will help me.

I Can Make Good Choices

1. I can tell my parents that I would like to help clean up after the disaster. I can pretend it is a treasure hunt and look for things of value to my family.
2. I can think about how strong our family is and that we have been through other hard experiences and that we will make it through this one.
3. I can ask for a night-light for awhile if I am scared. I won't always be afraid.
4. I can play earthquake with my friends again and again.

I Can Trust God to Be There for Me

Bible Verse: "Even though I walk through the valley of the shadow of death, I will fear no evil, for you are with me" (Psalm 23:4).

Prayer: Dear God, this has been such a hard time. Thank you for protecting me. Please help the other families that are sad and worried. Amen.

The child asking about the
NEW AGE

Understanding the Child

New Age concepts are frequently infiltrated throughout television programming, contemporary music, education, self-help groups, political platforms, comic books, toys, video games, and books. All children growing up in North America will be exposed to the ideas of the New Age, although they may not recognize that this belief system is in conflict with the teaching of Christian faith.

Much of the language of the New Age sounds similar to Christian teaching, so children may not initially understand how much in conflict they are.

Young children believe that all churches are essentially the same and differ only because of the churches location or type of building. By the time children are in Junior High School they are beginning to understand the essential beliefs of the Christian faith, and are able to exclude false teaching.

The essential focus of the teaching of the New Age is that man is his own god. In addition, New Age teaches that god is in everything and everything is god. The New Age denies that man is a sinner, and therefore denies the necessity of Christ dying for our sins. The New Age does not accept the Bible as the ultimate guide for living.

Children need to understand that New Age teaching and Christian teaching are opposite. They cannot both be true.

What YOU Can Do to Help the Child Understand the New Age

1. Tell children what the New Age teaches and how it is different from biblical teaching:
   a. New Age teaches that whatever a person decides is right, is right for him. There is no single standard for what is right or wrong that applies to everyone. Christians believe that what the Bible says is the only standard for right and wrong.
   b. New Age believes in reincarnation. Christians believe that after people die they either go to Heaven or Hell.
   c. New Age believes that people do not need the death and resurrection of Jesus Christ to be saved from sin. Christians believe that people are sinners, so Christ had to die for us.
   d. New Age teaches that god lies within everyone, and that people can become anything they want to become. Christians believe that there is only one true God, Jesus Christ.
   e. New Age believes in practices that are condemned in the Bible, such as spirit guides, astrology, crystal balls, horoscopes, channeling.

2. Tell children that the New Age has many beliefs that are good, but the reason for the belief is wrong. Some examples include:
   a. The New Age believes that we should clean up the environment (right), because god is in everything and everything is god (wrong).
   b. The New Age believes that we should accept each other (right) because truth is whatever a person chooses to believe (wrong).
   c. The New Age teaches that Jesus was a good man, as well as God (right), just like everyone is a good person (wrong).

Conversation Starters

"What did you think when your teacher said that all the religions of the world are true, and that people should believe whatever feels right to them to believe?"

"How can you decide whether something is true or not?"

"How can you tell other kids about your Christian beliefs in a nice way?"

"Not all Christian churches are the same and that's okay. How is Bob's church different from ours?"

"Does that movie teach that people don't really need God?"

Pointing the Child to God

Children need to know that God loves people who don't believe He exists.

TELL ME ABOUT THE NEW AGE

Why Is This So Confusing?

The New Age teaches that people are their own gods and that we don't need Jesus Christ to save us from our sins. Of course that's not true, but lots of people believe it. Since so many people believe in the New Age, you will see and hear New Age ideas when you watch TV or sometimes even from your teachers at school. If you know what the New Age believes, then you will know how it is different from Christian teaching.

The reason it is so confusing is that so many of the beliefs sounds just like what you have been taught as a Christian. The beliefs sound alike, but they aren't.

I can do all things through Christ who strengthens me!

What Does the New Age Religion Believe?

1. That Jesus was a good man, but not the only God. They believe that all religions are equal, so people can believe whatever they choose.
2. The New Age teaches that everybody goes to Heaven, even people who don't accept Christ into their hearts, and that there isn't any Hell.
3. They believe in reincarnation, spirit guides, past lives, astrology, and other things the Bible says are wrong.
4. The New Age believes that god is equally in every person and everything.

This is how I feel

_____

_____

_____

_____

I Can Help Myself

1. I can ask the Holy Spirit to help me understand the Bible.
2. I can read the Bible myself so I know what it says about Jesus.
3. I can remember that people who have wrong beliefs may be very nice people.
4. I can remember that becoming "empowered" or "developing my human potential" isn't possible without Christ in my life.

I Can Make Good Choices

1. When I hear something that doesn't sound like what I know the Bible says, I can ask my parents or Sunday school teacher about it.
2. I can help clean up the environment because God told us to take care of His world, not because I think that god is in all the plants and trees.
3. I will be kind to people who do not believe like I do, and pray for them, and talk about why I believe that Jesus is God, whenever I have a chance to do that.
4. I will refuse to read the horoscope in the newspaper or watch cartoons with spirit guides.

I Can Trust God to Be There for Me

Bible Verse: "Jesus answered, 'I am the way and the truth and the life. No one comes to the Father except through me'" (John 14:6).

Prayer: Dear God, thank you for sending the Holy Spirit who helps us know what is true and what isn't true. Amen.

The child affected by the
OCCULT

Understanding the Child

Children are exposed to the occult throughout childhood in a variety of ways, such as horror stories in movies, books, videos, Halloween, natural curiosity about mysterious and frightening events, jokes they hear about Satan, games such as Dungeons and Dragons or Ouija boards, music which honors Satan, and through New Age teaching at school which encourages beliefs in the supernatural, spirit guides, etc. In addition, children will learn about Satan at Sunday school, through reading the Bible, and by listening to family discussions.

The celebration of Halloween is controversial in some families because of the possible occult connection, but most Christian families do participate in Halloween activities. Young children want to be scared but not too scared. They enjoy learning that the monster is really their friend dressed up in a Halloween costume. Becoming a scary monster themselves allows children to feel powerful instead of weak. Parents who are casual and playful about Halloween will decrease excessive fears in children.

Children usually do not make a deliberate decision to affiliate with a satanic group until Junior High years. Christian children are more susceptible than children who have had no spiritual training because they have already come to accept the supernatural. In addition, children from Christian families know that alignment with a satanic group represents the ultimate rebellion against their parents.

Children most at risk for occult influence include those who come from divorced homes, have above average intelligence, feel alienated from peers, are highly creative, are fascinated with evil, and those who use alcohol or drugs.

What YOU Can Do to Help the Child

1. Do not allow the child to view blood-and-gore films which contain murder scenes at theaters or on videos.
2. Halloween parties should focus on fun not evil. Activities which include Ouija boards, witch costumes, fortune-tellers, tours of cemeteries at night, or hurting animals are not appropriate.
3. Do not allow CD's or tapes into your home without reading the lyrics first. Explain that words that encourage violence, suicide, or Satan worship are not acceptable and will be removed.
4. Allow children to trade in tapes and CD's of black metal music or music that contains other inappropriate lyrics for good tapes.
5. Make home an emotionally warm, happy place to live. The best way to avoid rebellion against Christian values is a loving, nurturing home where kids have fun.
6. Do not allow children to adopt any satanic group behaviors in your home: no T-shirts with inverted pentagrams, no black candles, Book of Shadows, skulls, occult posters, or painting one or two fingernails black.
7. Provide emotional closeness, physical affection, and involvement in school, sports, youth group activities. The child who feels special to his parents will have less need to feel special in a satanic group of rebellious adolescents.
8. Set limits and provide leadership. Don't allow disrespectful behavior to parents or siblings, profanity, lack of church attendance, nor the bedroom to be off limits to parents. Children do not need to read the Satanic Bible.
9. Meet your child's friends; know where your child is.

Conversation Starters

"No matter what kind of problem you have, we will always love you and try to help you. Can you tell us what is happening now?"

"Let's listen to your new CD and talk about the lyrics afterwards."

"I need to tell you that I am sorry about my behavior and ask you to forgive me. I love you and respect you."

"I'm so glad that you are in our family. I don't know what we would do without your good sense of humor."

"I see that your friend, Jessica, is wearing all black clothing and has died her hair black. She looks very unhappy. What could we do to show her that we love her?"

Pointing the Child to God

Children need to hear their parents praying for them and to feel cherished by their parents.

WHAT IS THE OCCULT?

Why Is the Occult Wrong?

The occult teaches that Satan is more powerful than he really is, and that many activities that God said are wrong are really okay. Christians follow the directions that God gave in the Bible to decide what is right or wrong. Some of the common activities of the occult that the Bible says are wrong include: being rebellious against parents, not going to church, swearing, lying about where you are going, thinking about evil rather than good, sneaking time with friends that your parents do not approve.

What Do Other Kids Think About the Occult?

There are many reasons why kids might be attracted to the occult. Lots of kids are simply fascinated by evil. Kids who do not feel accepted at home might be attracted to the occult because they want to be a part of a close group of friends where they can belong. Some kids are angry and get involved as a way of being rebellious. Sometimes it is hard for kids to understand what is wrong with wearing T-shirts with occult symbols or listening to black metal music since some of their friends do it. They say that it doesn't really mean anything bad. The reason it is wrong is that anything that does not honor God is wrong. Kids who get involved in the occult usually do it gradually.

This is how I feel

_____

_____

_____

_____

I Can Help Myself

1. I will spend time with people who make me love Jesus more.
2. I will pray for kids at my school who don't know Christ as their Savior.
3. I will memorize Scripture that helps me resist the temptations of Satan.
4. I will think about who I admire and what kind of role model I want to be for younger kids.
5. I will do the things that help me become all that God wants me to be. I will avoid the appearance of evil.

I Can Make Good Choices

1. I can listen to music that is clean and honors God.
2. I will look through my bedroom and remove anything that might have occult connection: tapes, posters, comics, clothes, jewelry, candles, skulls, Book of Shadows, etc.
3. I can decide to use the Bible as my guide for what I believe and what I do.
4. I will ask my parents or youth pastor how to make right decisions.
5. I will not play with Ouija Boards at parties and I will avoid excessively playing Dungeons and Dragons.

I AM THE WAY, THE TRUTH, AND THE LIFE Jesus

GOOD NEWS

I Can Trust God to Be There for Me

Bible Verse: "Put on the full armor of God, so that when the day of evil comes, you may be able to stand your ground" (Ephesians 6:13).

Prayer: Dear God, I know that I don't have to be afraid of Satan because you are more powerful than Satan. Amen.

The **OVERWEIGHT** child

Understanding the Child

Overweight children may be accused of being lazy, undisciplined, or ugly. It is difficult for overweight children to maintain a sense of self-worth in a society that places such high value on being thin.

In addition to damaged self-worth, overweight children may be more clumsy in athletics, and they have more accidents. They are more inclined to develop certain diseases. They may have difficulty finding clothes that fit social fads. And, they may experience teasing in the school cafeteria about their food choices.

Overweight children are seldom as popular as thin children.

Children may attempt fad diets or hunger strikes as a way to lose weight, but children should not attempt any diet without the supervision of a doctor.

One-third of children in the U. S. under eighteen are considered fat. Obesity is defined as 20% above average for the child's height.

Overweight is caused by eating more calories than the child needs and by lack of physical exercise. The tendency to gain weight easily, however, is often inherited. If both parents are overweight, there is an 80% chance the child will be overweight. Eating and exercise habits of the parents influence children as well. Boys are more likely to lose their baby fat than girls. The pattern for overweight may be set by the time a child is three years old.

Children may overeat in order to make themselves less attractive after they have been sexually abused.

What YOU Can Do to Help the Overweight Child

1. Give children control in appropriate situations. Children who have choices in life are less likely to overeat.
2. Tell children every day that they are loved, precious, valued. Affirm who they are, not how they look.
3. Gently explore the possibility of sexual abuse by inviting children to talk to you if they have a problem.
4. Demonstrate appropriate food intake and exercise, and avoid the use of food to reduce stress.
5. Don't allow high caloric foods in the house. Make low calorie snacks as attractive as possible.
6. Give children something to do or hold when they watch TV if that is a time when snacks are normally eaten.
7. Encourage recreation that includes activity. Take walks or ride bikes to interesting places.
8. Ask children if they are hungry when they ask for food. Overweight children need to learn to respond to internal cues, not eat simply because it is time to eat or because they are bored.
9. Ultimately, children control how much they eat, so avoid power struggles about food. When the child is motivated to lose weight, provide the support needed.
10. Help children develop healthy life-style habits, even if they never become thin.
11. Teach children how to deal with teasing about their weight.
12. Teach children how to make and keep friends.
13. Give children opportunities to earn money so they can buy flattering clothes.

Conversation Starters

"You deserve a reward. What special activity would you like to do?"

"You are a very good swimmer. Do you enjoy it?"

"Would you like to go with me to the hair stylist? Both of us could get our hair done."

"You may invite some friends to stay overnight if you like."

"Would you like my help in losing weight?"

Pointing the Child to God

Children need to know that God loves them just as they are, and that their body is the temple of the Holy Spirit.

I WISH I COULD LOSE WEIGHT!

Why Is This So Hard?

Maybe you have been teased about being overweight. If that has happened, I am sure that you felt very badly because you don't like being overweight and nobody likes to be called by unkind nicknames.

Maybe your parents are overweight too and no one criticizes you at home, but you feel uncomfortable when you are with kids at school or church. Even when kids try really hard to lose weight by doing everything they are told to do, it is still very hard. Some kids just gain weight easier than other kids.

Of course there are some very good reasons to lose weight, and there are some good suggestions to help you do it, so don't get discouraged. The most important thing to remember is that your worth has nothing to do with your weight. God will love you just the same whether you lose weight or not.

How Do Other Kids Feel?

Most kids wish there was some magical way to lose weight without having to give up their favorite foods or to exercise! Lots of kids who are overweight have a hard time in their P.E. class. They worry about how they look in their P.E. clothes and they have a hard time running. Kids who feel badly about themselves sometimes want to eat for comfort. Of course, that doesn't help the problem of being overweight.

This is how I feel

_____

_____

_____

_____

I Can Help Myself

1. I can learn to be a good friend and spend time with kids who are encouraging and nice. And I can learn what to say when others tease me about being overweight.
2. I can learn to develop my special talents so that I have lots of successes. If I am good at math, I will become the best math student I can be, and if I am good at swimming, I will swim as fast as I can.
3. I will ask someone to help me lose weight. It is too hard to do by myself.

I Can Make Good Choices

1. I can eat when I am hungry and stop when I am full. I won't eat just because other people are eating.
2. I will chew my food slowly and make each bite last a long time.
3. I can ask for a hug instead of food.
4. I can decide which physical activities I enjoy the most, and spend some time everyday playing hard.

I Can Trust God to Be There for Me

Bible Verse: "The Lord does not look at the things man looks at. Man looks at the outward appearance, but the Lord looks at the heart" (1 Samuel 16:7).

Prayer: Dear God, I am so glad that you love me exactly as I am. Help me to show that kind of love to others. Amen.

The child whose
PARENTS OFTEN FIGHT

Understanding the Child

Some children know more about fighting than they do about peacemaking. Violence in TV programming is frightening, but loud, angry, tense fighting between the adults they live with can be terrifying. Children know that they are dependent and cannot protect themselves. If the adults they love are out of control because of their anger, children feel very unsafe and in jeopardy.

All parents have disagreements, including strong arguments during the child's growing up years. Neither disagreements nor arguments are damaging to the child. Children need to know that grown-ups can strongly disagree with another person, talk out their differences and compromise. The only families which do not have verbal disagreements are those in which one parent is completely dominated by the other, and the subservient parent is afraid to speak his mind. Parents who use demeaning, threatening, hostile language in fighting, and who do not resolve differences, leave children untrained in knowing how to negotiate with others.

In addition, children are often the recipients of unresolved rage in their parents. Children are frequently spanked out of misplaced anger, not as a form of discipline intended to benefit the child. At times children are beaten because the care givers do not know normal growth and development, i.e. they may expect more from a child than he is capable of at a particular age. Boys are hit more often than girls.

Angry parents who hit their children produce children who hit their brothers and sisters. Sometimes children attempt to intervene between fighting adults and are accidentally injured in the process.

What YOU Can Do to Help the Child

1. Don't protect children from all adult disagreements. Be a model in talking about problems and respecting others opinions.
2. Tell children that it is not true that "those who love you are those who hurt you," as children may come to believe.
3. Teach children what to do if they are with their parents during a serious verbal fight. If very frightened, or either parent has been drinking alcohol, call the police and ask for help. Don't try to physically protect an adult.
4. Children need to know that they have permission to talk about the problems in their home. They do not need to protect their fighting parents by pretending everything is fine. It is okay to talk to a school counselor, a Sunday school teacher, or another helpful adult about what is happening.
5. Children need to know that adults are not always right, and that grown-ups may need to learn better ways of dealing with anger.
6. Children should be told that no matter what an angry parent might say, children are not the cause of fighting between parents.
7. Children who live with fighting adults are likely to have limited skills in expressing feelings. These children sometimes develop physical symptoms, such as tummy aches in response to tension in the home or as a means of diverting attention away from the parents fights.
8. In healthy homes, children should be told that even when parents are mad at each other, no one will be hurt.

Conversation Starters

"There is an old saying, 'Sticks and stones may break my bones but names will never hurt me.' That is not true. Do you know why?"

"What are some ways to express anger without hurting anyone?"

"What is the scariest part for you when Mommy and I have arguments?"

"What are you feeling right now?"

"When I was angry last night, I said some things that were hurtful and untrue. I need to learn better ways to deal with my anger. I am sorry. Can you forgive me?"

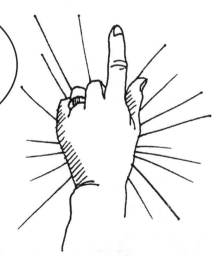

Pointing the Child to God

Children need to know that God cares about how family members treat each other and can help them live together in peace.

WHY DO MY PARENTS FIGHT SO MUCH?

Why Does This Hurt So Much?

It is embarrassing to tell anyone that there is a lot of fighting in your home, so perhaps you have never told anyone about the problem. It is okay to talk about it though. You don't have to pretend that it isn't a problem. It is normal to feel worried if adults are fighting. You might have worried that your mom would be hurt, or that you would be hurt. Maybe you just didn't know what to do.

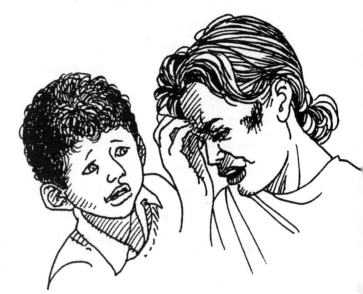

If there is lots of fighting in your home, you probably don't feel very good about yourself. That's why fighting hurts! Kids don't grow up knowing how to talk about their feelings, and work out their problems. They have to be shown and taught by grown-ups.

How Do Other Kids Feel?

Kids want their parents to like each other and to be polite and kind to each other. Nobody wants to live in a home where the grown-ups are fighting. Some kids think that there is something about the kind of kid they are that causes their parents to fight. But that is not true. Adult fighting is always the problem of adults. Kids need to know that anger is a normal feeling. Everyone is angry at times, and that what is important is what we do with our angry feelings.

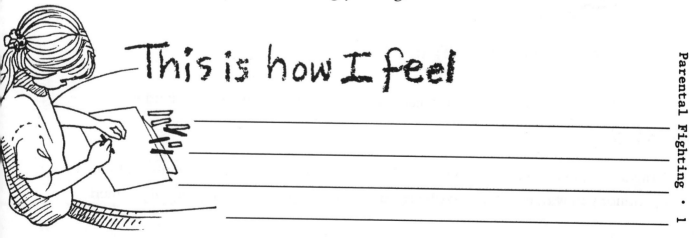

This is how I feel

_____

_____

_____

_____

I Can Help Myself

1. I can tell my parents how I feel about their fighting in a polite way.
2. When I feel angry, I can hit my pillow, jump up and down, talk about my feelings, ask for help, and think before I act.
3. I can turn to another channel if a TV program is violent.
4. I can learn the names of feelings so I know how to talk about them, including angry, sad, hurt, lonely, frightened.

I Can Make Good Choices

1. I can choose not to hit another kid if he hits me. Instead, I can walk away and talk to a helpful adult.
2. I won't try to stop my dad from hitting my mom, or even talk to my parents when they are in the middle of a fight. Grown-up fighting is a grown-up problem.
3. I can choose to make peace because that is what God wants me to do. If I don't know how to make peace, I can ask an adult who knows.
4. I can practice saying, "I am sorry. Please forgive me," so I'll be all ready when I need to say it!

I Can Trust God to Be There for Me

Bible Verse: "The Lord's servant must not quarrel; instead, he must be kind to everyone" (2 Timothy 2:24).

Prayer: Dear God, I know that you hear everything that is said in my family. Help me to honor you with how I talk to others. And, help my parents to stop fighting. Amen.

The child whose
PET DIED

Understanding the Child

The first time children experience grief is often the death of a loved pet. Young children are unclear about the meaning and permanence of death. It is hard for young children to understand that the pet is gone forever. If a pet's death is anticipated, children should be told.

Since grief is the natural response to losing someone or something the child loved, the death of a pet might be a profound loss. The sadness should never be minimized.

The pet should not be immediately replaced in an effort to protect children from emotional pain. The spiritual and emotional growth available for children after the death of a pet is the result of facing the pain, not avoiding it.

The grief work is likely to be impacted by the age of the child, how long the animal has been a part of the child's life, whether the child knew the death was coming, what the child is told about the pet's death, how much support is offered the grieving child, and most important of all, how much the child loved the pet.

Adults support children who are grieving a pet death when they themselves are free to cry openly and share their own sadness, and when they help children understand that grief is normal. It is the way anyone would feel who had lost a special friend.

Children will grieve in ways that fit their unique personality. No two children will grieve in exactly the same way. Children need to know that the way they are grieving is the right way for them.

What YOU Can Do to Help the Child Grieving a Pet's Death

1. Tell the child the truth about how the pet died. It is okay for the child to see the dead animal if it is not badly injured.
2. Give the child basic information about how the animal died, and then tell the child that you will answer any questions. Let children be in charge of what they want to know.
3. Recognize that the child may respond to the death in ways that are completely different from the parents' response. It is okay for parents to cry in front of children even if children do not cry.
4. Don't minimize the loss by finding something good about the death, i.e. "Fluffy was getting old anyway."
5. Don't push children to talk about their feelings. Invite them to tell how they feel, but trust them to do what they feel is best.
6. Young children communicate their grief through their behavior, not through words. What a child is doing is how he feels.
7. Don't buy a new pet right away. Let the child grieve and say good-bye to the pet. A new pet will not replace a former pet. Don't use the same name for a new pet.
8. Grieving children frequently lose their appetites for awhile.
9. Don't assume that children are over it simply because they resume play and activities. Children often grieve in bits and pieces over a period of time.
10. Don't talk about the child's grief to others but do express your own feelings by saying that the animal died and how sad you feel. Children need to observe your model of healthy grieving.

Conversation Starters

"Do you remember the day we brought your puppy home to live with us? I think you became best friends that day. No wonder you miss him so much!"

"I feel sad and mad that the car hit our cat. What feelings do you have?"

"What is the hardest thing about your gerbil dying?"

"Do you know any other kids who have had their pet die? How did they feel?"

"Have you decided to tell your friends yet about Bambi dying?"

Pointing the Child to God

Children need to know that God created every animal, and that He knows when every sparrow falls. He knows about this death.

MY PET JUST DIED

Why Does This Hurt So Much?

I imagine that you are feeling very sad now that your pet has died. Lots of kids say that their pet was a special friend and that they feel lonely, and angry and full of questions. Death is a hard thing to understand, so it is okay to ask questions. Grown-ups don't know all of the answers about death, but they will tell you when they don't know the answer.

Sometimes other people might not understand that your pet was such a good friend, and that it wouldn't fix everything to get a new pet right away. You have a right to whatever feelings you have. Most people want to help you. They just don't know what to do.

It is okay to play and have fun even though your pet died. It doesn't mean that you didn't love your pet. Playing is what kids do even when they feel sad.

How Do Other Kids Feel?

Kids have different feelings. Some kids cry and some kids never cry, even though they feel just as badly as the ones who cry. Nobody grieves in exactly the same way. The way you are doing it is the right way for you, even if it is not how others feel.

Some kids feel guilty because they think they caused their pet to die because they were bad and this is the punishment from God. God doesn't make pets die. Car accidents and old age and illnesses make pets die.

This is how I feel

_____

_____

_____

_____

I Can Help Myself

1. I can talk about my feelings and cry if I need to.
2. I can have a good-bye ceremony, and invite my family to bring flowers, and share memories about my pet.
3. I can tell grown-ups what makes me feel better.
4. I can write a story about all the things I loved about my pet and save it forever.
5. I can play hard and get my angry feelings out that way.

I Can Make Good Choices

1. I can hit my ball instead of hitting my brother.
2. I can read stories or watch videos about other children who had a pet die so I understand how they felt.
3. I can make a scrapbook with my pet's collar and pictures, and write the dates my pet was born and died.
4. I can thank God for giving me such a special friend to love and care for.

I Can Trust God to Be There for Me

Bible Verse: "He gathers the lambs in his arms and carries them close to his heart" (Isaiah 40:11).

Prayer: Dear God, help me to remember that you know all about how sad I feel. Thank you for making such a special pet and for letting us be friends. Amen.

The **PHYSICALLY DISABLED** child

Understanding the Child

Children with physical challenges are more able than they are disabled. They differ from other children with the same disability. All children are unique whether or not they have a disability. Children with disabilities are not necessarily more mature, courageous, brave or special, than other children, although these attributes are often attached to them or their parents. Disabled children are like other children of the same age in that they go to school, have friends, get the flu, play computer games, and enjoy winning at games.

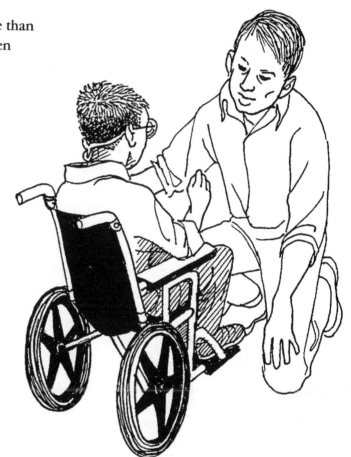

Children with disabilities do not want or need to be helped unnecessarily. All children, including disabled children, have gifts and skills that can enhance the lives of others. They can teach, share, support other children by using their particular areas of strength. Physically disabled children are not permanent victims.

Children who have been born with a physical disability may have less difficulty with their body image than children who acquire a disability later through an accident or disease.

Disabled children from Christian families may hear unhelpful comments which imply that if the family had adequate faith, the disabled child could walk again. Children may come to believe that the reason God didn't answer the prayer is because of some fault in them.

Disabled children need help in learning how to respond to invasive and personal questions, and able-bodied children need guidance in how to talk to a disabled child about the disability. Factual information reduces prejudice.

What YOU Can Do to Help the Physically Disabled Child

1. Ask the child about the disability. Ask what name the disability has, and what help, if any, the child wants from you.
2. Encourage the child to teach other children about the disability. Take the mystery away. Young children need to know that the disability is not contagious.
3. Focus on similarities, not differences, between children.
4. Learn about the special talents and skills of the disabled child and give the child an opportunity to help able-bodied children.
5. Tell the child stories about physically disabled children from the Bible.
6. Give able-bodied children direction about good manners with physically challenged children: don't stare; don't make public comments about the disability but ask the disabled person directly; don't be afraid.
7. Don't use the word crippled. It focuses on what the child cannot do instead of what the child can do.
8. Invite children with disabilities to your home to play.
9. Support brothers and sisters of disabled children. They may resent the extra attention that parents must give to the disabled sibling; they may feel guilty about their own freedom to play; they may be confused about what their parents expect from them in helping at home; they may worry about the future when parents are unable to take care of the disabled child.
10. Children with disabilities need perspective. All of us have limitations. Sometimes limitations show more than others. All of us need to maximize our potential.
11. Keep the focus on the child, not the disability.

Conversation Starters

"What do you especially like about Amy?"

"Could a child with a disability get into our church in a wheelchair? Into your Sunday school classroom?"

"What do you wish everyone knew about disabilities?"

"If you wanted to know about a particular disability, how could you get the information?"

"What could you do to be a friend to a child with a disability?"

"What are some ways that a child with a disability could help you? How could you help a child with a disability?"

Pointing the Child to God

Children need to know that some day, when we are in Heaven, no one will have any disabilities and that children who cannot walk now will be able to run.

I HAVE A PHYSICAL DISABILITY

Why Is This So Hard?

One of the reasons that it is hard to have a physical disability is that sometimes people don't take the time to get to know you. They might feel uncomfortable about the disability and be afraid to ask you questions so they can learn about it. That is too bad, of course, because even you had to learn about it once.

Sometimes people think that if you have a disability that you aren't as smart as people who are able-bodied. It is hard when people make judgments without finding out the truth.

Nobody wants a person to ask your parent, "What does he want?" when they could easily ask you what you want!

How Do Other Kids Feel?

Most kids with disabilities have some different experiences than kids without a disability. They may have been in the hospital for operations or physical therapy. Kids don't like to miss school or special events because they have to be in the hospital! Sometimes kids feel sad because they are limited from going some places other kids go because of their disability. It is hard for a wheelchair dependent student to take a power chair to the beach, or a blind student to attend a party at a video arcade.

Changing schools is usually hard for kids with disabilities. It takes awhile to feel accepted and to make friends with kids who are not uncomfortable with the disability.

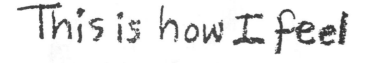
This is how I feel

_____

_____

_____

_____

I Can Help Myself

1. I can reach out to others and not wait for them to come to me. I can say, "It's not wrong to be curious about something you don't know. Would you like me to tell you about my disability?"
2. I can keep a good attitude, not take myself too seriously, and remember that God has a plan for my life just like He does for people who don't have disabilities.
3. I can remember that God requires me to be unselfish, to love and accept others, and to share, just as He does able-bodied kids.
4. I can learn to live one day at a time and know that God will help me in all of my tomorrows.

I Can Trust God to Be There for Me

Bible Verse: "Each one should use whatever gift he has received to serve others" (1 Peter 4:10).

Prayer: Dear God, I want to become all that I can be so that I will honor you with my life. Help me to use my gifts to praise you. Amen.

I Can Make Good Choices

1. I can encourage wheelchair access by writing letters to the editor of the newspaper and tell about locations that are difficult for wheelchair dependent people to enter.
2. I can plan something else fun to do when there is an activity I can't attend because of my disability.
3. I can learn some ways to serve and care for others who need me.
4. I can thank my brothers or sisters for helping me.

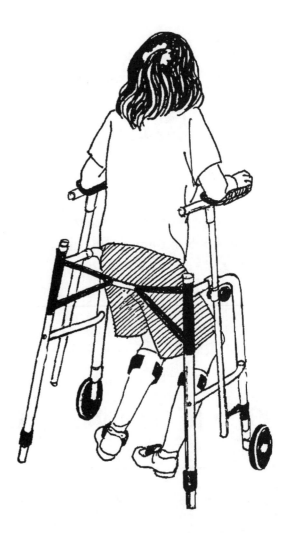

The child dealing with

POVERTY

Understanding the Child

Children live in poverty for a variety of parental reasons, including chronic mental or physical illness and inability to work; temporary unemployment; lack of work skills to get a job that supports the family; lack of willingness to work; drug or alcohol addiction; poor English language skills; illiteracy; unusual expenses such as occur with medical emergencies or a natural disaster; or simply the model of previous generations who lived on welfare and subsequent poor self-esteem to be assertive in acquiring a job.

Parents may feel guilty when children ask for things that they cannot afford to buy. It is helpful for parents to recognize that young children have limited ability to comprehend money and the costs of living. All children are self-centered to some degree, and need to learn the limits that will be set for them including the use of money.

Children will experience the prejudice that is often attached to people with low income. By the time children are in first grade, they know that rich children are favored and that having money results in power and control. Some people will assume that poor people are lazy or poor managers of money and that helping them financially will increase their dependence on donations.

Families with low income may not have medical insurance and children my not receive early diagnosis and treatment for ailments. They are more likely to be physically or emotionally abused due to the stress that lack of money creates.

Children who are not affected personally by poverty will usually have little knowledge about the difficulty of living on limited income.

What YOU Can Do to Help the Child Dealing With Poverty

1. Maintain respect and dignity and treat the child with courtesy.
2. Spend time with the child doing things that do not cost money even if you are willing to pay the expenses. Don't put the child in a position of always receiving help.
3. Teach children to prioritize their wants and needs and assist them with ideas to earn money.
4. Children with limited family income need to see or hear about others with less money and learn to assist them through church sponsored projects, assisting at shelters or at migrant worker camps, or through making needed items for the poor in other countries at Sunday school.
5. Children with low income still need to learn to save money consistently even in small amounts.
6. Build self-esteem in children that is not related to money. Teach children to excel in a hobby, sport, music, or academically.
7. Guide children into free cultural experiences, such as classical music, opera, reading good literature, learning another language. Show them how to access these materials through the library.
8. Teach children cost comparisons, "Those jeans cost as much as a new tire for a car."
9. Instill a strong moral base for acquiring and spending money. It is better to be poor than get money through gang affiliation and selling drugs.

Conversation Starters

"We don't have very much money, but we are going to make it. Let's talk about some of the ways we can get through this tough time."

"What are you worried about?"

"I have a friend who is very good at working with hair. Would you like her to cut and style your hair? It would be free."

"I respect your ability to save money for the things that you especially want. Would you like to do some jobs at my house and earn some money on Saturday?"

Pointing the Child to God

Children need to know that although having enough money is necessary, the best things cannot be bought. God's gift of his son, Jesus, is free for the taking.

WE DON'T HAVE MUCH MONEY

Why Is This So Hard?

You may feel that others judge you by how much money your family has, and if your family is having a hard time right now, you might feel embarrassed, worried, or sad. Lots of families have difficulty with money at times, so it is not unusual. Having little money does not mean that you are less important than someone who has lots of money. You don't need to apologize for not having new clothes or lots of toys when you invite friends over to your house. The reason they want to come over is to have time with you, not what you own.

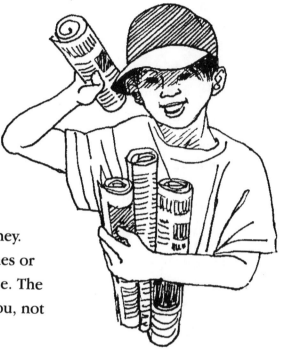

How Do Other Kids Feel?

Sometimes parents fight about not having enough money or how the money is spent. It is very hard for kids to hear their mom and dad arguing. Sometimes kids think they should sell their toys or find some other way to help the family get money. But that is not necessary. Kids can learn to earn the spending money they need and leave the big money problems for the adults to figure out.

Some kids, who live in families that do not have a lot of money, know they are the richest kids around because they have a family that loves each other and enjoys being together. Some rich kids are unhappy and some poor kids are happy.

This is how I feel

_____

_____

_____

_____

I Can Help Myself

1. I will think of alternative ways of getting the things that I want or need, such as shopping at a thrift store, accepting nice, but outgrown clothes from someone older than me, and giving my outgrown clothes to someone else.
2. I will develop hobbies that do not cost much money, such as collecting butterflies, singing, drawing, or building with scrap lumber.
3. I will plan how I want to spend the money I have earned by working, so I don't spend it impulsively.
4. I will talk to my parents about what it was like for them when they were growing up and what they learned about money.

I Can Make Good Choices

1. I can wait a day before I spend money on something. If I still want it, then I can go back and get it.
2. If your parents are fighting, ask if there is anything you have done to cause the problem. If they say no, then remember that adult problems are not kid problems.
3. I will write down all of the ways I can show someone I love them without spending money. At Christmas I can give gifts of my time to clean walkways or wash windows.
4. I can read stories in the Bible about what Jesus said about money.

I Can Trust God to Be There for Me

Bible Verse: "Command them to do good, to be rich in good deeds, and to be generous and willing to share. In this way they will lay up treasure for themselves" (1 Timothy 6:18-19).

Prayer: Dear God, some things that are not important seem too important to me, and I forget the things that are important. Please help to keep this straight. Amen.

The child with
PREJUDICE

Understanding the Child

Children are not born with prejudice. They learn it. By the time children enter kindergarten, they show a preference for playing with children of their same race. Children who are the recipients of early prejudice are not likely to understand why they have been excluded, but they will know that they are treated differently than other children.

Prejudice may be directed at low economic status, racial heritage, religious affiliation, disability, or old age. These biases will be communicated in TV programs, demeaning humor, and in overheard prejudicial statements by adults.

Intolerance of another person may make children feel superior. It is less likely to occur when they feel secure in themselves and are therefore less threatened by others. Self-confident children can accept differences in people better than insecure children.

Children who are excluded by prejudice have more difficulty succeeding academically, socially, and emotionally. They are more likely to act out in angry ways, to take fewer risks, and to develop prejudices of their own.

Children who live, work, and play together are less prejudiced. The most important factor both in preventing prejudicial attitudes and in supporting children who experience prejudice, is a kind, affirming, and unprejudiced parent.

Children who is are old enough to ask questions about prejudice need information. They should be told that prejudice is wrong. It is not acceptable as a Christian and will not be tolerated in the family. Hate will be met with love, acceptance, and accurate information. Being different does not mean being inferior or superior.

What **YOU** Can Do to Help the Child Understand Prejudice

1. Tell children that God loves and accepts everyone equally. Show respect for differences.
2. Teach children about cultural differences by reading stories about heroes of other races, eating in restaurants of other nationalities, and by learning other languages.
3. Invite children of other races over to play.
4. Don't assume that being equal means being the same. A minority child in a neighborhood will still be different.
5. Don't apply extraordinary pressure on minority children to succeed in an attempt to over compensate for stereotyped attitudes.
6. Teach children empathy by role playing experiences of prejudice at church or home.
7. Do not tolerate slang or stereotypes that are disrespectful of others.
8. Develop friendships with adults from other races as a model for children.
9. Provide dolls of other races so that children can nurture and have fun with them.
10. Seek help and service from persons of other races, i.e. go to a black dentist, have car servicing done by a Spanish-American, etc.
11. Point out the similarities, not differences, to children who have disabilities.
12. Don't assign chores at home by gender, or encourage career choice based on traditional stereotyped roles.
13. Tell children stories about your own grandparents and your respect and enjoyment of them.
14. Build self-esteem in children. Children who like themselves will like others more easily.

Conversation Starters

"What do you think about men becoming nurses and women working in a construction job?"

"How do you think that made him feel?"

"What would be one way you could show friendship to an elderly person?"

"Do you think that black students at your school are blamed for some problems before people really know who caused the problem?"

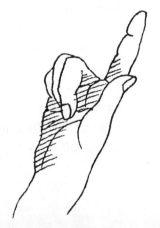

Pointing the Child to God

Children need to know that God is the One who decided to make all races and that since Jesus was born in the Middle East, He probably had dark skin.

DON'T REJECT ME JUST BECAUSE I'M DIFFERENT

Why Is This So Hard?

Nobody wants to be rejected based on their skin color, or how much money they have, or whether or not they have a disability. Everyone wants to be accepted as equal but unique from everyone else. If you have experienced prejudice, you have every right to feel badly about it.

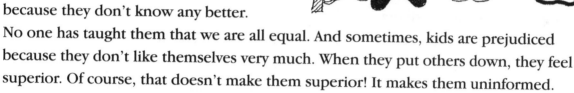

Sometimes other kids are prejudiced because they don't know any better. No one has taught them that we are all equal. And sometimes, kids are prejudiced because they don't like themselves very much. When they put others down, they feel superior. Of course, that doesn't make them superior! It makes them uninformed.

How Do Other Kids Feel?

Other kids know that there are outstanding leaders from every nationality and that the way one group of people does something doesn't mean that is the only way to do it.

Kids don't like it when others make generalizations about a race. For example, just because one black child is a good basketball player, it doesn't mean that every black child is good at playing basketball.

Kids can experience discrimination because of being overweight, disabled, not having much money, and a lot of other reasons.

This is how I feel

_____

_____

_____

_____

I Can Help Myself

1. When there are newspaper articles or TV stories about prejudice, I can talk about it or ask questions.
2. I can ask my parents about my family tree so I can learn about the original countries of my great-great grand-parents and find out what languages they spoke.
3. I can go to camp with children who are different from me.
4. I can be friendly and helpful to everyone, not just kids who are like me. When I see someone doing something well, I will say so.

I Can Make Good Choices

1. I can speak out against prejudice when I see it at school or in my neighborhood.
2. I will remember that it is no more acceptable to be especially nice to a rich kid just so I can play at her house, than it is to reject someone because she is poor.
3. When I hear an unkind slang expression about a group of people, I can ask for the correct way to describe them.
4. I can list all of the ways I am like my disabled friend.
5. I can read stories in the Bible about poor people loved by God, disabled people He helped, and people of other races He used.

I Can Trust God to Be There for Me

Bible Verse: "The Lord does not look at the things man looks at. Man looks at the outward appearance, but the Lord looks at the heart" (1 Samuel 16:7).

Prayer: Dear God, help me not to think that some people are more important than other people. I want to learn to treat people just like you do. Amen.

The child with

LOW SELF-ESTEEM

Understanding the Child

No child feels good about himself all of the time. Experiences that damage self-esteem can be offset with affirmation and competence in other areas. Children must be taught how to respond to failure in ways that maintain a sense of self worth. Children usually have good self-esteem until they begin first grade. From first grade through Junior High years, self -esteem gradually drops lower and lower. By the time children finish Junior High School, 95% of them state that they don't like themselves very much.

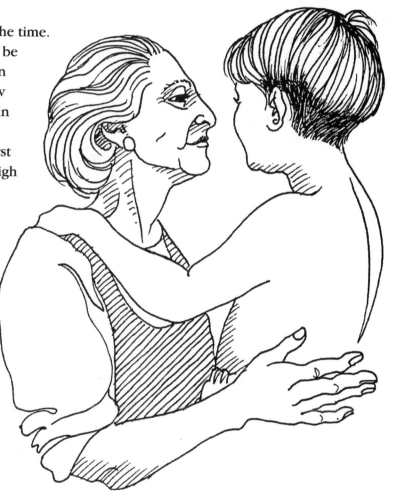

Children often decide their worth by external factors, such as how they compare to other children, or to media, and advertising. Children are constantly given non-Christian values for determining worth, such as the amount of money they have, whether they are beautiful or handsome, how smart they are, and whether or not they have athletic or musical gifts.

Children with low self worth feel helpless to recognize or develop their natural gifts. They tend to become frustrated and angry easily. They take fewer risks, and they select friends who are consistent with their low self-esteem.

Self worth becomes damaged by overly protective parents who do not allow children to develop competence by making mistakes and learning to handle failure casually. Self-esteem may also be damaged by adults who have unreasonable expectations of children and overly react to imperfection, or who excessively punish, or fail to provide one-to-one attention, leaving children feeling physically and psychologically worthless. The child's belief about his parents' assessment of his worth matters more than anyone else. Children need to feel their parents approval.

What **YOU** Can Do to Help the Child With Low Self-Esteem

1. Give children factual information about their behavior, but avoid linking their worth to the behavior. Children believe the statements made by adults. Say, "You failed the test," not, "You are a failure."
2. Spend time alone with the child daily. Look at the child's face while you listen. Hug the child ten times a day. Smile frequently. The amount of time you spend is less important than the quality of really being "with" the child.
3. Verbally express respect for the child's effort. Say, "We know how hard you have tried." Point out progress.
4. Teach children to be an expert at something that distinguishes them from others, such as leaning how to fish, sew, etc.
5. Casually refer to the child's strengths in conversation.
6. Tell children about your own past failures. Tell them the skills they have that you did not have at their age.
7. Show you are having fun playing games, even when you lose.
8. Teach kids how to make friends: apologize, share, compliment, take turns, etc.
9. Show children how to consider alternatives when faced with a problem, so they don't feel helpless.
10. Don't overly protect, encourage dependency, or allow excuses for not doing their best. No matter how difficult math is, the child's skill will improve with hard work.
11. Don't allow children to blame others for their failures.
12. Teach children how to respond to teasing or bullies.

Conversation Starters

"Did you have fun doing that project?"

"You can decide. Let's list the reasons for doing it on one side of the paper, and the reasons not to do it on the other."

"I love to hear you laugh. You really bring joy to our family."

"I love to hear about how your day was at school. Thanks for telling me about it. I pray for you while you are gone."

"Let's talk about how you can make some more friends. Would you like to invite someone over to play after school tomorrow? I'd be glad to drive them home."

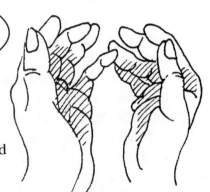

Pointing the Child to God

Children need to know that they have been created in the image of God and that God loves them more than they can possibly imagine!

LEARNING TO FEEL GOOD ABOUT YOURSELF

Why Do I Feel Like This?

Maybe you think that if you had lots of money, or if you were really good looking, or if you had some special talent, that you would feel good about yourself. The truth is, you do have some unique gifts because God gives everyone talents. You can learn to see yourself like God sees you. That doesn't mean that you will have a big head. It does mean that you will know the truth about how valuable you are. You will probably need some help in changing how to feel about yourself. It is okay to need help because you deserve it.

When you are weak in one area, you can learn to excel in another skill. Learning to feel good about yourself is very important because you will feel much happier than if you don't feel good about yourself.

How Do Other Kids Feel?

Lots of kids say that they don't feel very good about themselves, so you are not alone! Sometimes kids brag and act like they can do anything, but usually kids like that are covering up for not feeling good about themselves.

Kids who are weak in one area, can learn to excel in another skill. God wants kids to feel precious and loved, because they are!

This is how I feel

_____

_____

_____

_____

I Can Help Myself

1. I can learn to make at least one really good friend. Having one good friend is more important than having lots of friends that I don't know well and who don't know me.
2. I can ask my parents or teacher what special talents they think I have and how I can improve them.
3. I will be casual about failures. Everyone who has learned to do something well, had lots of failures first.
4. I won't say bad things about myself to anybody, including to myself. When I lose, I will remember that what is important is whether I am improving, not whether I win.

I Can Make Good Choices

1. I can spend time playing with a friend in activities that are not competitive and make me laugh.
2. I can learn to be kind to others, to encourage them, and to avoid being selfish.
3. I can talk to an adult, especially someone who makes me feel happy about myself, listens to me, and lets me try new activities.
4. I can work hard at learning how to do at least one thing well, such as building models or playing the piano.

I Can Trust God to Be There for Me

Bible Verse: "You are precious and honored in my sight" (Isaiah 43:4).

Prayer: Dear God, I want to believe what you say about me more than what anyone else says. Thank you for loving me so much that you sent Jesus, and that you live in my heart. Amen.

The child who is

SERIOUSLY ILL

Understanding the Child

Children with serious illness have usually experienced a number of traumatic experiences prior to
the present crisis. They have well defined fears of
injections, bone marrow aspirations, blood draws
by the lab, and fears of being left alone without
parents at the hospital. They are afraid of being
helpless in an adult-centered environment, and
older children are afraid of what the illness will
do to them.

Children are especially frightened by an illness
that affects their brain, genitals, heart, or eyes.

When death is a likely outcome of an illness, children
usually face the reality of death more quickly than their parents.
Children have an uncanny ability to sense when their parents are able to
tolerate talking about the possibility of death, and they wait until their parents
are comfortable before they are open themselves. When parents can talk about it,
children are usually ready. Parents and other involved adults who maintain a stiff
upper lip for the benefit of the child, leave children to manage their terror alone.

Prior to age six, most children are more worried about separation from their parents
at the hospital than they are about the possibility of dying from the illness.

Children do not know how they are supposed to behave in an Intensive Care Unit
where they have little control of the events that happen to them. Children soon
learn that if they don't hold still for injections, they will be held down.

What **YOU** Can Do to Help the Seriously Ill Child

1. Whenever possible allow the child to remain at home for care. Children always feel more secure at home.

2. Visit the hospitalized child regularly so that parents feel safe in going home to shower or rest while you are there.

3. Keep a journal of tests, medications, doctor's names and comments, and the child's response to treatments, as well as a journal of your own feelings. This log will be helpful as a reference in asking questions of doctors and as a written record of the child's illness.

4. Be honest with children. Another child may die at the hospital, the bone marrow test may indicate the leukemia has returned, but truth should always be presented with hope. Live in the present, not the future.

5. Don't be afraid to deny visiting rights to children or adults with colds.

6. Children love to receive mail, balloons, pictures of playmates, pets, and family. Decorate the child's room.

7. Join a support group of parents with children who have seriously ill children.

8. Tell the child when something will hurt and give some direction about what he can do to help himself tolerate the procedure, i.e. squeeze your hand as hard as he wants.

9. Assist the child in connecting emotionally with the medical care givers by helping her write thank you letters or draw pictures as gifts.

10. Give the child choices whenever possible so the child feels some sense of control.

11. Acknowledge that everyone who loves the child will suffer, including grandparents, cousins, school friends.

Conversation Starters

"You can decide what to wear today, what TV cartoons to watch, and whether you will call Grandma."

"Let's think of some things you can do when you feel scared or lonely ..."

"Is there anything you would like to ask the doctor today when we see her?"

"What do you think is going to happen?"

"I feel sad and upset because you are so sick, but I can still take care of you and help you."

Pointing the Child to God

Children need to know that God cares about everything that matters to them. He knows when a sparrow falls, and He knows when the child's hair falls out from chemotherapy.

BEING SICK IS NO FUN

Why Does This Hurt So Much?

Being sick is very hard! At first you probably didn't know what was the matter, but you knew your parents were upset and you had to go to the doctor a lot. You probably had to have a lot of blood tests, and maybe you had to stay at the hospital where you met a lot of strangers, had IV's, and took a lot of medicine. It probably felt strange at the hospital to sleep in a bed with side rails. One of the hardest things about being so sick is being separated from your parents during the times when they can't stay with you. And, of course, it is hard when you throw up or have pain. No wonder being so sick is hard!

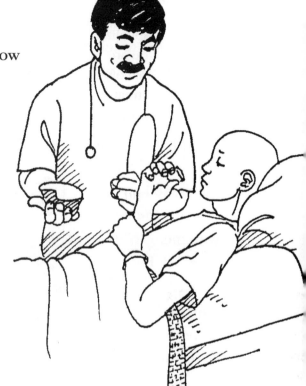

How Do Other Kids Feel?

Lots of kids think that their parents can protect them from all of the bad things that could happen. It is hard to find out that even though your parents love you very much, some bad, hard things still happen to kids.

Kids don't want to be different from other kids, so it can be embarrassing when chemotherapy makes their hair fall out and they have to wear a cap, or when they have scars from operations.

Kids don't like to be separated from their friends or to miss special events at school.

This is how I feel

_____

_____

_____

_____

I Can Help Myself

1. When I am lonely I will call my friends on the phone and talk or ask them to tell me something that will make me laugh.
2. I will decorate my room with pictures of my favorite people and things, so I always have my friends with me.
3. I will ask for a flash camera when I am in the hospital so I can take pictures of the nurses and doctors and my visitors.

I Can Make Good Choices

1. When I don't understand what is happening to me, or why I need a medicine or a treatment, I will ask.
2. I can teach my friends what they can do to help me. If I like it when my friends come to the hospital and help me put a puzzle together, I'll tell them.
3. I can ask to listen to my heart with a stethoscope or have an empty syringe (without the needle) to give shots to my teddy bear.
4. I can listen to a tape of my grandpa and my cousins and my neighbor telling me jokes even if laughing hurts my incision.

I Can Trust God to Be There for Me

Bible Verse: "Show me your ways, O Lord, teach me your paths; guide me in your truth and teach me, for you are God my Savior, and my hope is in you all day long" (Psalm 25:4, 5).

Prayer: Dear God, I am so glad that you knew me before I was born and you know what will happen every day of my life. Amen.

The **SEXUALLY ABUSED BOY**

Understanding the Child

Approximately one out of every four boys is sexually abused before they reach eighteen years of age. Until recently the problem has been largely ignored, which has left abused boys feeling very alone. Boys are taught that they must take care of themselves, so sexual abuse results in feelings of terrible shame.

Boys may be abused by men or women, people who are gay or straight, married, or single. Most sexual abuse of boys is by straight men. Boys who were abused by a male may have fears that they are now gay. The assault may or may not have been physically painful. The majority of boys know their abusers. Most boys will have great difficulty talking about their abuse experience, so very few boys will know that this has happened to many other boys.

Boys feel confused when they have an erection during the abuse and think that this means that they liked it. They must be told that their body responded automatically and that this does not mean they enjoyed what was happening.

Boys may be "groomed" by a potential sexual perpetrator so that the sexual abuse is accepted. This occurs when the adult treats the boy as special, gives extra attention, and arranges time alone with the boy. Initial touching is usually confusing and less blatant than it will be later. Beginning abuse may include casual touches while showering together or purposefully rubbing against the boy's body. Inappropriate teaching about sex or sexual displays of the adult's body are all a part of early sexual abuse.

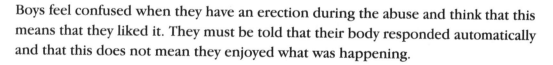

BAD TOUCH IS ANY UNWANTED SEXUAL TOUCH!

What YOU Can Do to Help the Sexually Abused Boy

1. Observe early warning signs that abuse is occurring: nightmares, increased aggressiveness, reenacting sexual behavior with other children, choking/gagging at meal times, complaints about being physically sick, finding reasons to avoid contact with a previously trusted person, and excessive masturbation.

2. Boys may believe that there is something unique about them that caused the abuse, or they may not know that the touching is wrong, or how to stop it. This shame makes it difficult for boys to admit that sexual abuse is occurring. Do not probe, but believe what the boy tells you even if you know and trust the abuser.

3. Perpetrators often abuse 70-125 children in a lifetime, so tell the child that the abuse needs to be reported to prevent the abuser from doing it again. This may encourage the boy to report it.

4. Read books about good touch vs. bad touch. Talk openly. Say "Bad touch is any unwanted sexual touch."

5. Focus on the type of touch that is wrong rather than the person who is doing the touching.

6. Tell the boy that adults are always responsible for their actions, and nothing the boy did caused the adult to abuse him.

7. Tell the boy that you feel angry because he was abused, but you are not mad at him. You know it wasn't his fault.

8. Tell children that it is wrong for a grown-up to ask a child to keep secrets from his parents.

9. Don't correct the child's language when he initially tells about the abuse, or it may appear coached when he reports it to the authorities.

10. Don't confront the abuser. Call the Children's Protective Services in your community or the police.

11. Don't smother the child with attention and imply that this is the worst thing that could ever happen.

"Kids can't know if what an adult is doing is okay. Have you ever wondered about something an adult was doing to you?"

Conversation Starters

"If anybody ever tells you not to tell your parents, then you know that what he is doing is wrong. You can tell us. We will understand and will not be mad at you."

"How can you express your anger without hurting anyone else?"

"I'm sorry I didn't realize what was happening to you. Now I see what you were trying to tell me by your behavior."

"What worries you the most?"

Pointing the Child to God

Children need to feel that God sees them as precious, clean, and loved. God is proud of them for exposing the abuse.

SEXUAL ABUSE IS HARD TO TALK ABOUT

Why Does This Hurt So Much?

If you have been sexually abused, you are probably feeling embarrassed about it, but sexual abuse is never the fault of the child. Even if you enjoyed the special attention that your abuser gave you, and even if it took you a long time to tell about it, it is still not your fault that you were abused. You told when you were able to tell.

You may feel badly that the abuser has gotten into so much trouble, but telling was the only way to make him stop the sexual abuse.

You may have to talk to a doctor or a policeman about the abuse. These are people who need to know about it so they can help you. Maybe you are not sure it was really sexual abuse because he never touched you, but he showed you sexual videos or exposed his private parts. That is sexual abuse, too.

IT'S NOT YOUR FAULT!

How Do Other Kids Feel?

Most kids feel confused and wonder why someone that they trusted would do something wrong. Lots of boys feel that they should have been able to protect themselves from the abuse. They are ashamed that they were tricked into the sexual touching and didn't report it right away. Some kids wonder if they are gay after having been sexually abused by a man, but the answer is "no." Having sexual touching with a man does not make you a homosexual. Kids worry about others finding out about the abuse, and they worry that people will be able to tell by looking at them that they have been abused. Only people who need to know will be told, and nobody can tell by looking at you that you were abused.

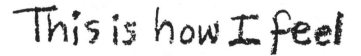

This is how I feel

_____

_____

_____

_____

I Can Help Myself

1. When I am not sure if an adult's behavior is okay, I can ask a safe adult, such as the school counselor.
2. If I was unable to tell about the sexual abuse or walk away, then I will remember that I told when I was able to tell.
3. I can give myself permission to cry and to love somebody while I'm still angry with them.
4. I can write a letter to the abuser. I don't have to mail it if I don't want to.

I Can Trust God to Be There for Me

Bible Verse: "Jesus said, 'Let the little children come to me, and do not hinder them, for the kingdom of heaven belongs to such as these'" (Matthew 19:14).

I Can Make Good Choices

1. In the future, if an adult tries to sexually touch me and I am too scared to tell him to stop, I can say that I have to leave and then get out of there!
2. I can learn the correct name for all my body parts, including the sexual parts, so that I can talk more clearly about what happened.
3. I can accept my angry feelings at my parents for not protecting me from the abuse. I know they didn't know that it was happening.
4. I don't have to explain what happened to everyone who asks. I can say, "I just talk about that with my mom."
5. I can choose to forgive the person who hurt me. I know that forgiving doesn't mean that what happened to me was okay, but I can let God deal with the abuser.

Prayer: Dear God, I know that you can help me with all of my angry, sad, mixed-up feelings right now. Thank you for being a Friend who will never, ever hurt me. Amen.

The SEXUALLY ABUSED GIRL

Understanding the Child

One out of every three girls is sexually abused before eighteen years of age. Sexual abuse often begins when a girl is eight years old and then lasts three or more years.

Usually a girl is not forced to participate in sexual activity with an adult. The abuse is based on a gradual, trusting relationship with an adult who knows the child, and has power over the child. Girls may be seduced by gifts, attention, or favors.

Both men and women abuse little girls. Abuse may occur with a parent, grandfather, step-parent, or boyfriend of the mother. Abusive fathers may be overly protective of a favorite child or overly authoritarian. They sometimes tell the child, "Your mother knows about this and said it was okay." Many abusive fathers have low self-esteem and poor relational skills. They do not get their needs met with other adults. The abuse usually takes place in the home of the offender of the child.

Clues that a girl is being sexually abused include: frequent physical complaints, changes in mood, sexual behavior in play, difficulty sleeping, excessive masturbation, sexual knowledge beyond her years, desire to avoid a previously liked adult, difficulty concentrating at school, regression to more immature behavior, bed-wetting, restlessness, withdrawal, or extreme shyness about her body.

Most girls will make repeated attempts to communicate that they need help before an adult responds with assistance.

What YOU Can Do to Help the Girl Who Has Been Sexually Abused

1. Be alert for nonverbal behavior that sexual abuse might be occurring and make yourself available to listen without judgment. Say, "Sometimes kids have a problem and don't know how to get the help they need. If you ever need to talk to a grown-up, I would be glad to listen and help you."

2. Report disclosure or strong suspicions of sexual abuse to the police or the state Children's Protective Services. You can remain anonymous unless it goes to court, but that rarely occurs.

3. Be emotionally warm and calm as you listen to the child. Hysterical or angry adults frighten children.

4. Say, "I believe you. I know that you wouldn't lie about something like this."

5. Don't confront the offender. Leave that to the authorities.

6. Don't talk about the abused child to anyone who does not need to know the information in order to help.

7. Girls who are being sexually abused blame themselves for the abuse. Tell a girl that nothing she did made this happen.

8. Talk about good touch vs. bad touch, but remember that some sexual abuse does not involve touching (adult nudity, watching porno films, etc.).

9. Gently explore reasons why a girl does not want contact with a former trusted adult.

10. Don't ask for details when a child discloses abuse. She will have to repeat her story many times to the authorities.

11. Anticipate that the girl may feel angry at the parent who did not offend her. She may be ashamed and feel dirty, different, alone, and worthless. Build self-esteem by spending time with her that is not related to the abuse.

Conversation Starters

"I know that this is hard to talk about, but none of this is your fault. You can tell me anything you want, and I will love you and help you."

"Can I give you a hug?"

"Would you like me to read a story to you about another little girl who was abused?"

"Sometimes when girls have been sexually abused, they feel confused because they love the person who abused them and are angry with him at the same time. Is that how you feel?"

Pointing the Child to God

Children need to know that God can help them to feel good again, and that the bad feelings they have now won't last forever.

WHY DID THIS HAPPEN TO ME?

Why Does This Hurt So Much?

Sexual abuse happens to many other girls, so you are not alone. Maybe an adult in your family said that if you told about the abuse it would really hurt the family, or the police would take your father away, or you might have to go live in a foster home. That would be very scary to hear.

You were in a very difficult situation that was hard to talk about. You may have enjoyed the special attention that the abuser gave you, but of course you didn't want to be abused.

How Do Other Kids Feel?

Sometimes girls feel ashamed that they didn't tell about the abuse sooner, but it was too difficult to talk about it because they loved and trusted the person who was abusing them. Most of the time girls didn't know that what was happening to them was abuse. Maybe the adult said, "I'm just teaching you about sex." Girls thought that their mothers or other adults could tell by looking at them that the abuse was happening and would help them, but usually other adults didn't know what was happening.

Kids don't know how to forgive someone who abuses them. They think that forgiving means that what the person did was okay, but it doesn't mean that at all. To forgive someone means that you decide not to hurt the abuser for what he did to you, and then you get on with finding the help you need to be happy.

This is how I feel

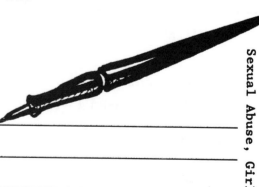

_____

_____

_____

_____

I Can Help Myself

1. I won't expect the person who abused me to apologize for the abuse or even to admit that what he did was wrong, because that might not ever happen.
2. I can be patient with myself and not expect to feel okay right away. Feeling happy again takes a while.
3. I can remember that there are many good, kind people who love me and will never hurt me. I can trust them to help me.
4. I can remember that I deserve help because I am loved by God.
5. I can learn the name for body parts so that I can use correct language to explain what happened.

I Can Make Good Choices

1. I can talk about my feelings to a counselor. If it is too hard to put my feelings into words, I can draw a picture to show how I feel.
2. I can say "no" to any touch that I don't want.
3. I can ask for help when I don't feel safe in the future.
4. I can ask for help in deciding who should be told about the abuse. I don't need to tell all of my friends about it.

I Can Trust God to Be There for Me

Bible Verse: "So do not fear, for I am with you; do not be dismayed, for I am your God. I will strengthen you and help you" (Isaiah 41:10).

Prayer: Dear God, this has been such a scary, hard time for me. Thank you for being close beside me to help me. And thank you for sending good people to be my friends right now. Amen.

To protect the child against
SEXUAL ABUSE

Understanding the Child

Children who are constantly told about the dangers of sexual abuse become frightened. These necessary warnings must be balanced with affirmation that there are many good adults who can be trusted to be helpful to children. In addition, children must be given clear direction about what they can do to protect themselves when threatened with sexual exploitation.

The most important protection against sexual abuse that parents can provide children is close, frequent, warm communication. Children who feel safe and loved are less vulnerable to being seduced by other adults. Sexual perpetrators can spot children who are lonely and in need to adult attention.

Sexual perpetrators often seek contact with young children through volunteer roles in clubs, Sunday school classrooms, or in school settings. An adult who sexually abuses one child will abuse many, many others.

Since strangers commit only about 10% of child sexual assault, it is not helpful to limit warnings to "stranger danger." Young children think of a stranger as someone who is frightening. An unknown, but friendly person is not a stranger. The focus of prevention is in teaching children about wrong behaviors by any adult.

Children who are comfortable talking about sexual topics, will be far more likely to disclose any questionable behavior by an adult. Adults should initiate these talks and present information in a casual, comfortable way.

What **YOU** Can Do to Help Prevent Child Sexual Assault

1. Avoid discussing frightening details about what might happen to children who are sexually assaulted.
2. Tell children that they are not responsible to help adults who ask for directions or who seek assistance in locating a missing pet. Adults ask adults for help.
3. Teach children that no adult is to touch them in the areas covered by bathing suits, except for necessary cleaning by their parents or by medical care providers. And children are not to touch adults in private areas.
4. Children can be taught that it is good to be polite and friendly to strangers. They do not need to be afraid of people they don't know, while at the same time teaching them to follow the rules about not allowing inappropriate touch or actions.
5. Children need to know that it is okay to say "no" to inappropriate behavior by an adult.
6. Talk to children in a calm, matter-of-fact way. Instill confidence that the child can make right choices.
7. Know where children are, know their friends, know their daily routine, and their usual route home from school.
8. Teach children the correct names for all body parts, including sexual parts, so that if they need to tell about wrong touch, they can describe it accurately.
9. A four year old is old enough to know his home phone number, how to call for help in an emergency, and how to place a collect call.
10. Be alert to a teenager or an adult who is paying an unusual amount of attention to your child or buying them special gifts.

Conversation Starters

"Let's pretend that I am an adult who asks you to do something that feels wrong. What could you do?"

"What are some of the things that make you feel afraid?"

"Your opinions matter to me. How did your time with the new baby-sitter go last night?"

"You are very nice looking. If someone asked to take your picture, you can say, My parents don't allow someone I don't know to take my picture. I need to ask them first."

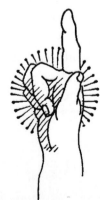

Pointing the Child to God

Children need to know that God is with them wherever they go and when they feel afraid they can talk to Him.

WHAT IS SEXUAL ABUSE?

Why Is Sexual Abuse Wrong?

Sexual abuse is any unwanted or wrong sexual behavior by a grown-up with a child. Sometimes this includes touching children in their private parts, or taking pictures of children without their clothes on, or uncomfortable kissing, or watching dirty videos with the child, or talking in a sexual way. Sometimes an adult asks a child to touch him, or shows his private parts to the child. Sexual abuse includes other behaviors as well. If you are not sure that an adult's actions are wrong, you can ask a trusted adult because sexual abuse hurts kids, and you deserve help in knowing how to be safe!

Sexual abuse is any unwanted or wrong sexual behavior by a grown-up with a CHILD!

How Do Other Kids Feel?

Kids might not know that they have the right to say "no" to an adult, especially if the adult has been very nice to them. Usually sexual abuse is confusing and the kids don't know what is really happening before it becomes clear that the behavior is wrong. Then, lots of kids feel embarrassed and worried that someone will think they made this happen, but everybody knows that kids can't make adults do wrong things!

Some kids think that only bad strangers would hurt a child by sexual abuse but that isn't usually the case. It might be done by someone that kids know, so it is important to learn what actions are wrong and what to do when they happen.

This Is What I Would Do If Someone Tried to Sexually Abuse Me

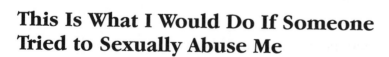

_____

_____

_____

_____

I Can Help Myself

1. I can talk to my parents if someone touches me in a way that feels confusing.
2. If a grown-up asks me for directions, I can say, "You need to ask another adult."
3. I can refuse to keep wrong secrets from my parents.
4. I can remember that although my parents love me and want to protect me, they can't always be there. I can learn to protect myself in many situations.

I Can Make Good Choices

1. I will not play or walk home from school alone. I will stay with other children.
2. I can say "no" to an adult if he touches my body in a way that makes me feel uncomfortable.
3. I can decide to never get into a car with someone other than my parents unless my parents have given me permission. Even if someone says, "Your Mom said for me to bring you home," I won't ride with them unless I have permission from my parents.
4. I won't talk to other adults about sexual questions without the permission of my parents.

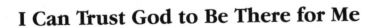

I Can Trust God to Be There for Me

Bible Verse: "It is God's will that you should be sanctified: that you should avoid sexual immorality; that each of you should learn to control his own body in a way that is holy and honorable" (1 Thessalonians 4:3).

Prayer: Dear God, thank you for providing loving adults who want to help me. Please keep me safe. Amen.

The child living with a
SINGLE PARENT

Understanding the Child

Children may live in a single parent home due to the death of a parent, or because the parent has never married, or as a result of divorce. Whatever the circumstances, children mourn the absence of two parents.

Even when the family was very unhappy prior to a divorce, most children do not see divorce as solving the family problems. The child's grief may last several years, long after the single parent has adjusted to living apart from the former mate. As children become accustomed to life with only one parent, each child in the family will respond to the change differently.

Younger children need much reassurance that the parent who does not have custody is still their parent, and leaving the marriage does not mean that the parent left the child.

Some of the loss that children feel results when children are asked to assume responsibilities that are not required of children in two parent homes, such as being asked to give advice to their parent about dating, car purchases, or vacations.

Children who have regular contact with the non custodial parent are generally emotionally healthier than children who do not. In addition, when household rules remain the same in both homes, children feel more secure.

Children who live with their single mother may worry about family finances, since many single mothers have a loss of income.

Children in single parent homes sometimes become a confidant for their custodial parent. This too results in a loss of childhood.

What YOU Can Do to Help the Child

1. Recognize that some reactions to the absence of one parent may not be apparent for years, i.e. difficulty in trusting God and others.
2. Maintain predictable structure in the home. Don't let children sleep with you, stay up late regularly, or give advice about your dating.
3. Allow contact with relatives of the non custodial parent, such as grandparents, if the child desires it.
4. Discuss your financial concerns with another adult, not the child.
5. Agree with the non custodial divorced parent to avoid difficult discussions during pickup or drop-off times.
6. Give children permission to have a good time with the non custodial parent without upsetting you.
7. Talk to children about your dependence on God for wisdom to meet your family's needs. Pray together.
8. Don't allow rude verbal behavior from children because you feel that living in a single parent home has harmed them.
9. Don't ask your child to report on the behavior of the non custodial parent after visits, i.e. who she is dating, etc.
10. Provide time with an adult of the non custodial parent's gender. A boy who lives with his mom needs a male soccer coach, or male Sunday school teacher, etc.
11. Encourage play, school activities, friendships. They will all be a part of the child's healing.
12. Help children figure out ways to earn extra spending money if it is needed. It makes them feel less helpless.

Conversation Starters

"Is it hard to tell me that you like your dad's girlfriend? You don't have to protect me. It is okay to like her, and it is okay to have fun with your dad."

"Do you think this TV show about a single parent family is telling it like it really is? What are they not telling?"

"Some kids feel angry, worried, or sad when they live with only one parent. What other feelings do kids in single parent homes have?"

"Lots of kids live in single parent homes. Do you know some kids in your room at school who live with one parent?"

"Sometimes children wish their parents would not date, but that is a grown-up decision. I do care about your feelings though. Do you want to talk about it?"

Pointing the Child to God

Children need to know that they can talk to God about all their feelings, not just the good feelings.

I WISH I COULD LIVE WITH BOTH PARENTS

Why Is This So Hard?

Maybe you have more responsibility than you used to have, and you wish you could just go out and play more. If your parents are divorced, maybe you wish you had a choice about going to visit your other parent on the weekend.

Maybe you feel jealous of kids who live with both parents. Maybe you wonder if you will always feel sad, and scared, and mad. Lots of other kids have felt this way too, but you won't always feel like you do now!

How Do Other Kids Feel?

Some kids say that they feel pretty confused when they talk about their other parent, because it upsets the parent they live with, so they don't know what to say or not say.

Some kids say there are some good things about living with a single parent, like feeling really close to your custodial parent. When parents divorce, kids worry about things they never thought about before, such as will my parent get married again, and what will we do if the custody check doesn't come before I need new basketball shoes, and will I have a divorce when I grow up?

This is how I feel

_____

_____

_____

_____

I Can Help Myself

1. I can plan ahead to buy things. I can save the money I earn on Saturday to get the special shoes I want.
2. I can ask for help with my math if I have a hard time concentrating at school.
3. When my dad asks personal questions about my mom, I can ask him to talk to my mom about that.
4. I can love my mom and my dad.
5. I can memorize a Bible verse about how God takes special care of kids who live with only one parent.

I Can Make Good Choices

1. I can ask my mom if I can play in Little League so I can be around the great coach.
2. I can tell my friends that kids can be happy in two parent or single parent families.
3. I can read about God's plan for marriage and family.
4. I can give myself permission to cry when I need to.
5. I can learn how to solve problems when I am mad by reading stories about kids who solved problems.

I Can Trust God to Be There for Me

Bible Verse: "God sets the lonely in families" (Psalm 68:6).

Prayer: Dear God, thank you for protecting and providing for me in my single parent home. Thank you for your promise to help me live like you want me to live. Help me not to worry and to trust you more. Amen.

The child who lives with a
STEPPARENT

Understanding the Child

By the time a remarriage occurs, children have been enjoying the special bond with their parent which often occurs in single parent homes. The threat of losing that status to an intruder, however nice the person may be, is a major adjustment. It is hard for children to like someone who takes over their turf!

Children may find the stepparent very likable in any role but that of a parent! The resistance that children feel is the result of feeling threatened and not having the power to change the situation.

Initially, stepparents may spend extra time playing with the children of their new mate, which increases jealousy for the biological children. Birth order often changes when two single parents marry. The oldest child who becomes the youngest has many adjustments.

Children feel that if they love the new stepparent, they are betraying their noncustodial biological parent.

Moving to a new home may mean changing schools and neighborhoods and finding new friends.

Children don't know how to introduce their new step siblings. Initially these step siblings don't feel like bothers and sisters.

Physical affection, kissing, flirting between parents are all normal and healthy behaviors in a new marriage but may be embarrassing to older children.

What YOU Can Do to Help the Child

1. Biological parents can discipline their own children for the first year. When this parent is gone, the stepparent can say, "I am acting as your parent now."
2. Don't try too hard to make children like you. The bond cannot be rushed.
3. Recognize that fighting between parents in the stepparent home is often especially frightening since it makes children wonder if another divorce will occur. Tell them that all parents have disagreements. It doesn't mean we're getting a divorce.
4. Give children direction about what to do when they want to invite both biological parents to special events, "We know you would also like to invite your dad and his wife. You can make the decision that is right for you."
5. Family nights once a week are helpful and offer a time to talk about the concerns of everyone in the family.
6. Talking about how holidays are to be celebrated and combining the best of both families' traditions will help.
7. Telling children that you know they already have a mother and that you would like to become their friend, takes some of the confusion away regarding the stepparent's role.
8. At times stepparents may avoid facing their own problems by blaming stepchildren for all of the family difficulties.
9. Don't criticize nor defend the noncustodial parent. Allow children to make up their own minds.
10. Don't expect bonding to occur rapidly or automatically. Becoming a family will take much time and effort.

Conversation Starters

"What do you wish we knew about stepparent families?"

"Your mom and I are spending an evening alone tonight, then we would like to plan a fun evening for all of us. What would you like our family to do together?"

"What do you like/not like about our stepparent family?"

"I was wondering if you would like to spend the afternoon shopping with me? I'll get a baby-sitter for the other children."

"Getting used to a new stepparent family takes time for most kids. We don't expect you to get used to it right away. Is there anything we could do that would make it easier?"

Pointing the Child to God

Children need to know that honoring their stepparent is one way to honor God, and that they make God happy when they respect and obey their stepparent.

I HAVE A STEPPARENT

Why Is This So Hard?

In a new stepparent family there is sometimes more fighting than usual as everyone adjusts to living together. This is scary, but usually it won't last long.

Sometimes the stepparent is used to having different rules than you had before. It takes time for parents to agree on what the rules will be and who will tell kids what to do.

It is hard to share your parent with new stepbrothers and sisters when you have had your parent all to yourself.

It is hard to learn to live with sisters if you have only had brothers, and it is hard to have to share your toys with others when you have had them all to yourself.

How Do Other Kids Feel?

Kids have different feelings depending on how old they are when their parent remarries, how long they have know the stepparent, and whether or not they have had time to learn to like the stepparent before the marriage.

Lots of kids worry that it will make their noncustodial parent feel sad if they like the new stepparent.

In the beginning most kids don't like it when their stepparent tells them what they can or can't do.

This is how I feel

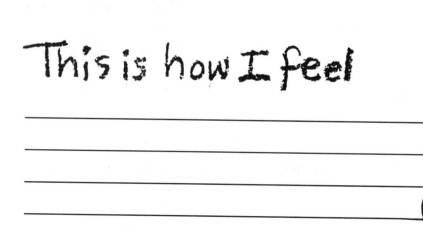

_____

_____

_____

_____

I Can Help Myself

1. I can tell my stepparent how I feel in a respectful way.
2. I can make suggestions about what I think would help our family, such as kids exchanging bedrooms every six months so nobody has the smallest room all of the time.
3. I can thank my new stepparent and stepbrothers and sisters when they help me, because I know this makes God smile.
4. I can ask for time alone with my biological parent.
5. I can ask questions and not assume something is true until I have checked it out.

I Can Make Good Choices

1. I can choose to keep an open mind about my new stepparent family and give myself time to adjust.
2. I can be obedient and helpful so that I don't cause any difficulty in my family.
3. I can write a list of all the good things about my stepparent family and thank God for them.
4. I can decide how much I want to tell about my visits to my noncustodial parent.
5. I can refuse to take sides if my biological parents have a disagreement.

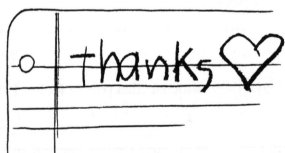

I Can Trust God to Be There for Me

Bible Verse: "Children, obey your parents in the Lord, for this is right" (Ephesians 6:1).

Prayer: Dear God, I'm glad that I never have to figure out how to solve my problems all alone, and that you want to help me become strong and happy in my stepparent family. Amen.

The child dealing with
SUICIDE

Understanding the Child

When a loved person commits suicide, children are left with a legacy of guilt, shame, and confusion.

Adults may be so intensely preoccupied with the event, that the needs of children are minimized.

Children may grow up believing that suicide is an acceptable option for dealing with difficult problems, or that suicide is somehow inherited.

Children have great difficulty comprehending that someone would choose to die. The sense of abandonment in a non accidental death is monumental. The child must not only grieve the loss of the presence of that person in their lives, they must acknowledge that the person made a deliberate decision to leave them.

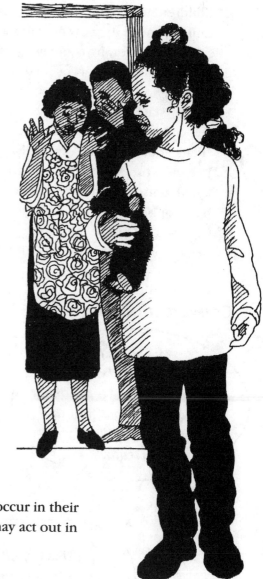

Children may inadvertently find the dead body and carry this painful traumatic memory for a lifetime. The most common means of committing suicide for a man is the use of a hand gun so finding the body is frequently terrifying.

Since young children believe that they cause the events that occur in their families, they will assume responsibility for the suicide and may act out in ways that invite getting punished.

Most people who commit suicide are depressed, and children may have lost quality relationship with the person as they withdrew prior to the actual suicide.

What YOU Can Do to Help the Child

1. Support children on the anniversary of the suicide since some children make a suicide attempt themselves, "to be with the person who died."
2. Tell children that there is always help available for people who feel like committing suicide. Suicide causes problems, not resolves them.
3. Tell children about suicide hot line telephone numbers. Show them where the number is listed in the phone book.
4. Children need to know how to resolve sad, lonely feelings, and learn to express them.
5. Children need to know how to locate helpers for people who are thinking about suicide, such as a doctor, psychologist, policeman, hot line, school counselor.
6. Offer physical comfort by holding and hugging the child. Verbally offer yourself, "I am here for you."
7. Clearly state that nothing the child did caused the suicide or could have prevented it.
8. Tell children they do not have to talk about the suicide to curious outsiders. They can say, "I talk about this with my family."
9. Use the word "suicide." Don't create a myth about why the person died. Say, "Uncle Joe killed himself because he didn't know that there were people who could have helped him," or because "He didn't accept the help that was offered."
10. Children should be told that in looking back, people can think of ways they could have helped prevent the suicide, but that everyone did the best they could at the time.

Conversation Starters

"No one in the family will lie to you about what happened. If there is anything you wonder about, you can ask me and I will tell you the truth."

"Do kids at school ask you about the suicide?"

"I feel sad that she wanted to die, and I feel angry that she hurt us by her suicide. How do you feel?"

"Let's think of all the ways he could have found help for his problems."

"Do you know what the word suicide means?"

Pointing the Child to God

Children need to know that because God created us, every person is precious to God, and suicide is never an acceptable answer to painful feelings.

WHY DO PEOPLE KILL THEMSELVES?

Why Does This Hurt So Much?

If someone you knew and loved committed suicide, you are probably having a very hard time right now. Sometimes grown-ups are too upset to explain what happened and why it happened, and you wonder if there is anyway you could have prevented the suicide. The answer is, there is nothing you could have done to stop it! There are many people who can help when a person feels desperate, alone, and sad, so anyone can get help if they want it.

Sometimes adults have a hard time talking about the suicide, so you are not sure if you should talk about it either. The truth is, kids who talk to someone about their questions and worries usually feel better than kids who don't talk about them. You won't want to talk to everyone who asks about it, but find a safe person and talk to them.

How Do Other Kids Feel?

Lots of kids feel ashamed when someone in the family commits suicide because the adults may try to hide the truth about what happened. A suicide sometimes becomes a bad family secret. It is hard for kids when grown-ups are very angry and upset, which often happens after a suicide. Kids aren't sure what will happen next. Kids feel better when they under-stand some of the reasons why someone might make a choice to commit suicide (such as mental illness, depression, not making good friends, abusing alcohol or drugs, etc.).

This is how I feel

_____

_____

_____

_____

I Can Help Myself

1. I won't keep bad secrets. If someone tells me that they are thinking about hurting themselves, I will say, "I'm sorry but I can't keep that kind of secret" and then I will tell an adult right away.
2. I can ask for help when I feel sad inside.
3. I can memorize Bible verses that tell how much God loves me.

I Can Make Good Choices

1. I won't try to make my family admit it was suicide. I know it is just too hard for some people to talk about.
2. I can learn the clues that someone might be thinking about suicide and tell an adult helper. Some clues are: a friend seems very sad, talks about dying, had a big loss, doesn't want to be with friends, or does dangerous things that might make them die, such as running into a busy street.
3. I can be a friend to someone who needs a friend.

I Can Trust God to Be There for Me

Bible Verse: "Let us then approach the throne of grace with confidence, so that we may receive mercy and find grace to help us in our time of need" (Hebrews 4:16).

Prayer: Dear God, I feel sad and mad about the suicide. I know that the life of every person is precious to you. Thank you for all the people who are willing to help when someone feels like committing suicide. Amen.

The child living with an

UNEMPLOYED PARENT

Understanding the Child

The loss of parental employment is a stressful event for children as well as their parents. Whether or not the issues are openly discussed with children, children feel the enormous tension and fear of their parents. Adults usually respond to the loss of income as they might to any other major loss, such as death or divorce. When parents are preoccupied with anger at the circumstances of the job loss, when others accuse them of causing the job termination, when they fear for the potential loss of their home or car due to inability to make payments, and when they resent the injustice and unanswered why of the job loss, children will also grieve but usually have less support than is provided their parents.

Fear in parents is terrifying to dependent children. Angry adults may displace their frustration on children. Children cannot distinguish realistic statements from those spoken out of anxiety, such as "If this lasts much longer, we'll be sleeping on the street."

Job loss places stress on marriages, and parental separation may occur. Or Mom may go to work to support the family on a lower income, and Dad feels like a failure in his inability to support the family. Since seeking employment is full-time work, both Mom and Dad may be less available to care for children. The average length of time for an unemployed parent to find a job with a salary comparable to the one that was lost is nine months. The average length of time for unemployment financial benefits is six months.

Many families are only one paycheck away from the inability to pay their bills. Unemployment causes major stress for the entire family.

What YOU Can Do to Help the Child Experiencing Parental Unemployment

1. Give general information about family finances and tell children specific adaptations the family will make to the reduced income.
2. When possible, include positive aspects of the job loss. "This is going to be hard, but Daddy can be trained for a new job."
3. Teach and model delaying gratification. Leave credit cards at home when shopping. Require a "cooling off" period before making impulse purchases.
4. Allow children to help by working to earn their own spending money. Avoid burdening children with the need to take care of parents' financial needs.
5. Create an elegant but inexpensive home atmosphere by using candlelight at dinner.
6. Plan specific ways to help the needy. Whatever the family income, children need to give to others.
7. Maintain health insurance if possible; utilize free sources of medical care for children, such as seeing the school nurse.
8. Adults should talk to adults about their fears and angry feelings. They should listen well to children and allow them to express their hurt without guilt.
9. Have family meetings once a week to talk about priorities in spending money. Help children find alternative ways of getting needs met.
10. Plan family fun activities which include everyone, and do not cost money, such as going fishing, playing in the snow, taking a hike.
11. Discuss Christmas shopping. Be creative. Suggest that everyone make at least one gift for family members. Attend free Christmas services; go to the woods for a tree. Give sentimental gifts of family heirlooms.

Conversation Starters

"Do you have any questions about Daddy's job loss?"

"Would you like to walk to the library with me and pick out some good books and videos?"

"We love you so much. You are worth more than a million dollars to us."

"When we go to the grocery store, let's see who can find the best bargain on food items we need."

"We are going to make it as a family."

Pointing the Child to God

Children need to know that God can provide for physical needs as well as spiritual needs and that He sometimes uses surprising people to meet our needs.

MY DAD LOST HIS JOB

Why Does This Hurt So Much?

Sometimes parents don't talk about family finances with their children, so if one of your parents is unemployed, you might not know very much about how that job loss will affect the family. It is okay to ask what changes might occur so it won't come as a surprise.

Maybe your parents say, "We can't afford that," every time you ask for something and you feel angry or frustrated. Maybe you are worried that your family is falling apart and you think you should do something to fix it. Usually kids can't do anything about unemployment though. You probably want to know about the best way to get along during this hard time and to be reassured that you are safe and loved.

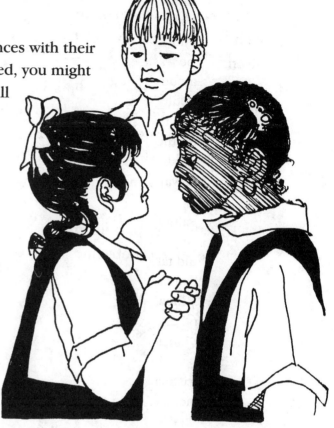

How Do Other Kids Feel?

One of the common reasons that a parent loses a job is due to new technology. Sometimes kids have more technical skills than their parents, such as more famil-iarity with computers. Kids may work at a fast food restaurant and be the only family member with a job. When that happens there is sometimes a change in roles between parents and children. Dad stays home and children go to work. Sometimes parents have to go to school to learn the skills that children already have. Parents who are used to being in charge may feel so sad after losing a job that they have a hard time setting limits for kids. Usually that makes kids feel insecure.

UNFAIR!

This is how I feel

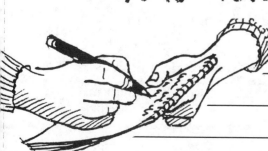

_____

_____

_____

_____

I Can Help Myself

1. I will ask for information about our family's money and then not feel guilty spending the money I am given.
2. I will pray for people who have less than our family.
3. If my parent is angry, or crying, or worried, I will ask if I caused it. If not, I will let grown-ups help my parent.
4. I will ask what steps our family will take to solve our problems.

I Can Make Good Choices

1. I can help by suggesting ways that our family can save money, and by encouraging my unemployed parent.
2. I can write in my diary about what has happened to our family since my parent lost the job. If my parent is getting more irritable, I can express my feelings in my diary.
3. I can help my mom learn to use the computer.
4. I can remind myself that this hard time won't last forever.

why cant I have what all the other kids have, Grandma?

I Can Trust God to Be There for Me

Bible Verse: "Do not be anxious about anything, but in everything, by prayer and petition, with thanksgiving, present your requests to God" (Philippians 4:6).

Prayer: Dear God, you know all about what is happening in our family right now. Please help my parent to find a good job, and help me to make good choices about how I spend my money. Amen.

The child with questions about
UNWED PREGNANCY

Understanding the Child

In some areas of the United States one in four babies is born to an unwed mother. Many children will know someone who is unmarried and pregnant. Children who attend Sunday school or are a part of a Christian family will sense the shame and embarrassment that may be attached to an unwed pregnancy. The child who is a part of the family may feel that this disapproval includes him.

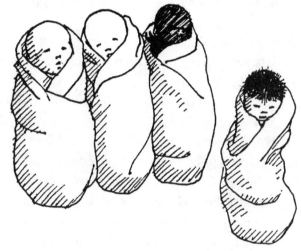

Parents who have avoided talking with their children about sex before marriage, or have not explained God's plan for sex, can read Christian books on sex education, seek direction from their pediatrician, and talk with other parents about how to present the information to their children.

Children are interested in sex and their questions are usually asked out of curiosity rather than morality.

Children need to understand the seriousness of raising a child while unmarried: The baby will likely have to be in child care while the mother works; most unwed mothers do not have enough money; most fathers of unmarried teen-age mothers leave the mother so she must raise the child alone; unmarried teens will have a hard time finding time for the normal fun of growing up while being a good parent.

Children can learn two important Christian principles: God gives people the ability to wait for sex; and He forgives people who sin, including unwed mothers.

What YOU Can Do to Help the Child

1. Attitudes are contagious. Adults who pray for the unborn baby and support the mother, while being clear that God's plan is that every baby is born into a family where the mom and dad are married, demonstrate Christian values.

2. Young children need to understand that they are to be kind to unmarried mothers. It is not okay to say, "Why aren't you married?" Or "Where is the Daddy?" Or "My folks said people shouldn't have babies when they aren't married."

3. Tell children what you believe about pregnancy outside of marriage while watching TV shows with this story line.

4. Don't wait until there is a family member or acquaintance who is unmarried and pregnant to talk about the issue. The topic should be brought up by parents of all children in grade school.

5. Tell children that it is not okay to have an abortion to terminate an unwanted pregnancy.

6. Tell children that raising a baby alone is difficult, and that Christians help unmarried parents.

7. The option of adoption should be explained to children, including the sadness of releasing a baby; but that loving a baby means doing what is best for the baby.

8. Children need to know that the only birth control method that is 100% effective is abstinence from sexual intercourse prior to marriage.

9. Grade school children need to know that it is easy to become like the people they spend time with, and that one way to avoid wrong sexual decisions is to be with friends who want to obey God.

Conversation Starters

"Have you ever known anyone who was an unwed mother?"

"She is pregnant but not married. If you have any questions you want to ask about that, I will be glad to answer them."

"Why do you think someone might get pregnant who isn't married?"

"What do you think our family could do to help our neighbor who is pregnant and not married?"

"Sometimes a girl gets pregnant because she doesn't think a guy will like her if she doesn't have sex with him. What could a girl do to change her bad feelings about herself?"

"Why do you think God told us to wait until we are married to have sex?"

Pointing the Child to God

Children need to know that God loves the unmarried mother and her baby, and we are to love them too.

WHY ISN'T SHE MARRIED?

Help Me Understand

Maybe someone you know is pregnant, but they aren't married and you are wondering what to think about that. I'm glad that you asked, because God has a lot to say about babies, and sex, and marriage. He also tells us how we are suppose to act around unmarried pregnant people.

It is okay to be curious and to ask questions. God made sex interesting!

God said that we are not to have sex with anyone before we get married, so when someone is pregnant and they aren't married, they have sinned. God doesn't love them any less though, and He always forgives everyone who is sorry about breaking God's law and asks God for forgiveness.

How Do Other Kids Feel?

If someone in their family is pregnant but not married, kids might have mixed feelings. They might feel excited because a baby will be born, and they might feel worried because people in the family are upset that the person isn't married. Or they might feel embarrassed because it proves that the pregnant person was having sex and that is a hard subject to talk about. Kids usually wish that their parents would talk to them about what happened and not just talk about it to other adults.

This is how I feel

_____

_____

_____

_____

I Can Help Myself

1. Sometimes grown-ups have a hard time talking about sex, so when you have questions, don't wait for them to bring up the subject. Go ahead and ask!
2. Learn all that you can about how parents take care of a baby. It will help you understand why it is so hard for an unmarried mother to raise a baby alone.
3. Talk to an unmarried mother and ask her about parenting alone. Would she recommend that people get married first before having a baby?
4. Think of ways to help an unmarried mother.

I Can Make Good Choices

1. I can ask God to help me always obey Him and thank Him for giving me rules that help me be happy.
2. I can decide to not have sex before I am married.
3. I can say "no" when friends ask me to do anything that my parents or God have said not to do.
4. I can spend time with friends who also want to make right choices and follow Christ.

I Can Trust God to Be There for Me

Bible Verse: "God is faithful; he will not let you be tempted beyond what you can bear" (1 Corinthians 10:13).

Prayer: Dear God, help me to remember to treat unmarried pregnant people like you would treat them. Amen.

The child affected by TV
VIOLENCE

Understanding the Child

All children are exposed to violence. Children observe thousands of murders on television during their growing up years. They watch violent cartoons, observe news reporting of local and international acts of aggression, and are enticed by advertising to buy toys designed to pretend they can hurt others by guns and swords.

Young children recall scenes of violence on TV longer than nonviolent scenes, and they react with fear. Some families limit sexual programming on TV but not stories with violence. The more violence that young children are permitted to observe, the more likely the child will be to use violent means of solving their own problems, especially children who have a tendency toward violence.

Children who are repeatedly exposed to violence are children who are inclined to be frightened, worried, suspicious. The child most at risk for reenacting violence is the one who has observed violence at home between his parents. Children who live with adults with short fuses, and who frequently yell and fight lack a model for resolving difficulties without force. They are more inclined to do to others what has already been done to them.

Some children are by nature more sensitive to exposure to violence. In addition, children do not interpret violence in the same way that adults do. They have little concept of time and distance. They do not know that street fighting in a city across the country is not nearby, or that horror stories are not real. Children believe in a logical cause and effect. People who are hit are those who deserve it for some reason. It is safer than believing that violence may occur randomly.

What YOU Can Do to Help the Child Affected by TV Violence

1. Tell children that violence on television is pretend and is done by actors to tell a scary story. Be casual and calm.
2. State that the war and fighting is in another part of the world and that bombs can't reach the child's house.
3. Watch the entire television episode of a series before allowing children to watch subsequent programs.
4. Talk about violence. Explain that some people don't know how to solve problems without fighting. Explain that there are other and better ways to resolve differences. Explain how violence hurts people.
5. Read stories about children who cooperate and care for each other.
6. Children sense the fear of their parents more clearly than they will believe the words they say. Parents who are terrified of street crime will have difficulty reassuring children.
7. Allow children to express their feelings and fears through play, but set clear limits on re-enacting violence that hurts others.
8. Limit television watching to one hour a day. Once viewing habits are established, they are difficult to change. Screen video films.
9. Tell baby-sitters what is, is not acceptable to watch on TV. Don't use TV to keep kids occupied.
10. Verbally express respect for people who keep their cool under pressure. Model what you want your child to learn.
11. Plan TV watching by the week using a program schedule.

Conversation Starters

"Let me explain the movie rating system and which movies our family watches ..."

"What other ways could those fighting kids use to solve their problem?"

"How did it make you feel when Jason said those mean words to you?'

"When you are in an angry situation, you can say firmly, I don't want to fight, but I will talk about the problem, or you can just walk away and deal with it after you feel calmer. Which would be the easiest for you?"

Pointing the Child to God

Children need to know that anger is a God given emotion, and that God will help them channel their anger so that no one is hurt.

TV VIOLENCE — FASCINATING AND FRIGHTENING

Why Is This So Hard?

It might be hard for you to know the difference between what is real and what is just pretend. Sometimes stories that are just pretend seem very real and you might have nightmares after watching a violent TV show. Another thing that is hard about watching violent TV shows is that you never really know how real people feel after violence actually happens. You might worry about whether the same kind of thing could happen in your neighborhood. Lots of times, violence goes together with using bad language, and treating women in disrespectful ways. God cares about what we see, and He wants us to follow His guidelines for how we treat other people.

How Do Other Kids Feel?

Sometimes the world feels like a scary place to kids who watch a lot of violence on television. Kids are fascinated by violence as well as being frightened by it, and that is why so many cartoons and movies are violent. Usually these films don't teach kids about helpful things to do when they are mad. Kids who watch a lot of violence sometimes hurt smaller children or pets or break their toys.

All kids and adults get mad at times, but there are ways to express anger without anyone being hurt.

This is how I feel

_____

_____

_____

_____

I Can Help Myself

1. I can remember that God is stronger than anything I fear.
2. When I feel afraid, I can tell a grown-up and ask him to help me. I can ask for a hug.
3. I can turn the TV off.
4. I can deliberately think about something good, funny, or happy when I feel upset by violence on TV.

I Can Make Good Choices

1. I can play hard outside with my friends, or be creative inside, instead of watching TV.
2. I can write a play and get my friends to act out the parts instead of watching a play someone else wrote.
3. If a bully picks on me, I can say, "Stop it," and walk away. If someone is much bigger than I am, I can talk to an adult about what happened.
4. I can read stories about people in the Bible that God loved and protected from danger.
5. The fact that someone treats me in an angry way, doesn't mean that I have to respond in the same way. Others are not the boss of how I act.

I Can Trust God to Be There for Me

Bible Verse: "I will fear no evil, for you are with me" (Psalm 23:4).

Prayer: Dear God, help me to watch TV shows that will make you happy with me. I want to please you by what I see, what I hear, and how I spend my time. Amen.